HISTORY OF ORANGE
North Milford
CONNECTICUT

1639 - 1949

BY MARY R. WOODRUFF

THE
CONNECTICUT
PRESS

Reprinted with corrections 2011
Published by the Orange Historical Society and
The Connecticut Press

Inquiries should be addressed to:
The Connecticut Press
135 Church Street
Monroe, CT 06468
www.connecticutpress.com

Cataloguing-in-Publication Data

Woodruff, Mary R. (Mary Rebecca), author
  History of Orange, North Milford, Connecticut, 1639-1949
  xiv, 177 p., 24 cm. Bibliography. Includes index.
  First printing 1949; Reprinted with corrections 2011
  ISBN 978-0-9825468-4-0 (paperback)

  1. Orange (CT) — History —1639 - 1949 2. Connecticut — History — 1639 - 1949 3. United States — History — 1639 - 1949 3. Connecticut — Genealogy — 1639 - 1949

  I. Woodruff, Mary R., 1876 - 1973   II. History of Orange
  ISBN 978-0-9825468-4-0
  Library of Congress Control Number: 2011922760
  LC Classification: F104.O7 W6   LC Shelving No.   974.67

Front Cover: (Clockwise from bottom left) Orange Congregational Church, 1810, designed by David Hoadley; Bryan-Andrew House, ca. 1750; Stone-Otis House, ca. 1830 (all three are listed on the National Register of Historic Places); and the 1871 New Haven & Derby Railroad Station on Orange Center Road. This Scobie postcard shows visitors on their way to the Orange Country Fair, ca. 1908. Centerpiece: Armorial of the Stuart monarch for use in England, 1603 onwards.

PREFACE

The *History of Orange, North Milford, Connecticut, 1639 - 1949,* by Mary Rebecca Woodruff, was the joining of the histories of the original Colony of Milford, established in 1639, and the section known as North Milford, later incorporated as the Town of Orange in 1822. At the town meeting held in March, 1946, Miss Woodruff was the unanimous choice to write the town's history. A lifelong Orange resident from a prominent family, she was the daughter of Stiles D. Woodruff, founder of S.D. Woodruff & Sons Seed Company. A tall, stately woman, who commanded the love and respect of all who knew her, Woodruff loved local history and was an active member of the Daughters of the American Revolution for most of her long life.

A pillar of the Orange Congregational Church, Miss Woodruff served on the Missionary Committee and as recording secretary for the annual meetings for more than 30 years. Her skill in drafting detailed reports was legendary for her flair in describing otherwise ordinary events. Having to put the details to paper for the history of her beloved town was a monumental task and an obvious labor of love.

Miss Woodruff's keen mind served her well as author of the *History of Orange.* Over a four-year period she conducted dozens of interviews, consulted countless histories, manuscripts, photographs, and old family papers in compiling the 300-year-old story of Orange. The result is a bona fide treasure that has served to introduce generations of Orange residents to their town's rich history.

Much has transpired since the *History of Orange* was first published. One thing that has not changed is the pleasure of holding this gem of a book in your hands, turning its pages as they were originally printed and making new discoveries as a result of owning your very own copy of this irreplaceable history. While this reprinted edition includes some corrections in the form of footnotes by railroad historian Robert J. Belletzkie, First Selectman James Zeoli, and myself — as well as new photos and a biographical sketch of Mary R. Woodruff by historian Peter J. Malia — the book remains faithful to Woodruff's 1949 classic.

The Orange Historical Society wishes to thank the many Woodruff family members who have graciously shared so many wonderful facts of their beloved Mary. We especially thank the Orange Foundation and the O'Sullivan Family Fund for their financial support and dedicate this reprinted edition to Tom O'Sullivan and Eleanor Pfeiffer.

Ginny Reinhard, President
Orange Historical Society - 2011

MARY REBECCA WOODRUFF
(1876 - 1973)

There is just a hint of a smile on the face of 15-year-old Mary R. Woodruff in her graduation day portrait from Orange High School in 1891. Her wry expression bordering on a smirk speaks volumes to the impish nature of a young lady whose spirit of independence earned her a lasting reputation as a force to be reckoned with by her family, friends, and community.

Mary is best remembered as the author of the *History of Orange*. But there is so much more to this woman's own personal story.

Born on November 3rd in the nation's centennial year of 1876, Mary was a child of privilege, wealth, and prominence. The only daughter of Stiles D. Woodruff and Elizabeth Clark, Mary's social standing seemed to predetermine her future course. Initially that meant attending Wesleyan Academy in Massachusetts in preparation for her matriculation at Oberlin College in Oberlin, Ohio as an arts and sciences student in 1897. The school's Presbyterian origins,

Mary R. Woodruff, above, at age 15 (see class photo, p. 61).

missionary zeal, and long support of social causes no doubt appealed to young Mary's own belief that to be good you must also do good.

After only one year at college, Mary inexplicably left her studies and never returned. Still, her Oberlin experience – epitomized by the school's motto of Learning and Labor – perfectly mirrored her own approach to life and she never forgot the school. Years later she even made a small donation to the college.

Once back in Orange, Mary pursued her interests in history, missionary work, and public service with an unequaled passion that saw her eventual rise to leadership positions in several national, regional, and local organizations. Among them were the Daughters of

iv

the American Revolution; the Order of the Founders and Patriots of America; the International Order of the King's Sons and Daughters, a Christian service organization; and the New Haven and Connecticut Federation of Women's Clubs, where Mary served as president and became a headline speaker on topics ranging from international relations and the world peace movement of the 1930s to planned parenthood and preventing marijuana use in the 1940s and 1950s.

Mary's penchant for writing also blossomed from her fledgling efforts as the author of a few short articles she penned for historical magazines just after the turn of the 20th century. By the 1930s, the *New York Herald Tribune* awarded Mary a ribbon for editorial excellence as a contributing writer to the *Connecticut Club Courier,* the official women's club magazine.

Mary R. Woodruff as she appeared in the New York Times *on May 17, 1942, on her election as president of the New Haven Woman's Club.*

 Mary's 'Connecticut Yankee' upbringing could also not help but highlight her practical nature as a talented business woman and tireless civic booster. At the urging of her brothers, she served as treasurer and a director of the family-owned Orange Water Company from 1911 until the Woodruffs sold the company in 1937. While she would always remain involved with family, church, and community in Orange, Mary set her sights on a broader horizon. Already living a non-traditional life, unmarried at 47 and destined to remain so, she moved to downtown New Haven in 1923. Living on her own at addresses on fashionable Chapel, Dwight, and Norton streets, Mary was busily engaged in social, civic, and writing activities for the next half century. Dignified and self-confident, she also traveled the country visiting family and attending various conferences, often as a featured speaker.

Finally, we come to Mary R. Woodruff the historian. Most scholars avoided writing local history in the first half of the 20th century because they felt it was too narrow a field to tell the American story. Even the Federal Writers Project of the Great Depression era bypassed Orange, most likely because of its small size. But the town's selectmen knew a good story when they saw one and they also knew just the writer to tell that story. Mary Woodruff's national notoriety, sense of community spirit, depth of knowledge about her local heritage, and her proven writing abilities made her the ideal candidate to author the *History of Orange.* From scholars to schoolchildren, we all owe this remarkable and distinguished first citizen of Orange a long overdue debt of gratitude for a job well done.

Mary passed away on February 18, 1973 at the age of 96. She came home to the town she brought so much honor to and rests in the Orange Center Cemetery.

Peter J. Malia

TOWN
of
ORANGE

FOUNDED
1822

HISTORY OF ORANGE
NORTH MILFORD

CONNECTICUT

1639 - 1949

COMPILED BY MARY R. WOODRUFF

1949

PRINTED IN U.S.A.

PRESS OF

PAYNE AND LANE

BUILDERS OF BOOKS

NEW HAVEN, CONNECTICUT

CONTENTS

ILLUSTRATIONS

Mary Rebecca Woodruff (1876 - 1973)
The above portrait was taken in 1971.

FOREWORD

In the opinion of Mr. Wilson H. Lee, as well as others, it seemed desirable that a history of the town of Orange should be compiled. In fact, the children of the eighth Grade of the Orange Center School felt it so keenly that they did some research work themselves, and presented it in a very creditable manner when they graduated from the Grammar School in June, 1946.

At a Town Meeting held in October, 1945, Spencer Hoyt, Paul Wright, Edward L. Clark, and Wilson H. Lee were appointed a committee to consider the subject. This committee presented a favorable report at the Town Meeting held in March, 1946, and recommended that the Selectmen be authorized to have such a book published, and that the material be assembled by the present writer. This recommendation was adopted.

The person most eminently fitted to compile such a record was Edward L. Clark, but he was not physically able to attempt it. He graciously allowed his manuscript of recollections to be used, and without his valuable help and suggestions, this story could hardly have been written. It is most deeply regretted that he did not live long enough to check it for historical accuracy. A great debt of appreciation for their valuable fund of facts and anecdotes is gratefully acknowledged to the following persons: Mrs. Frederick C. Sperry, Mrs. Charles S. Clark, Mrs. Henry H. Peck, Arthur D. Clark, Walter S. Hine, Dwight E. Russell, Mr. and Mrs. Benjamin T. Clark, Mr. and Mrs. Albert M. Clark, and Robert J. Woodruff. Since West Haven published a history of that part of the town in 1940, this volume is confined, exclusively, to the northern part of the town.

Many histories, manuscripts, and old family documents have been consulted, a list of which appears in the back of the book. As far as possible, proof of the accuracy of the statements herein made has been confirmed.

John Lowell once said, "Even though virtue and not descent is important, it is surely a strong motive to good conduct that your predecessors have done worthy service to the state." So this brief history is humbly submitted, hoping that it may arouse some sentiment of pride and the debt of gratitude we owe to the sober, industrious trail-blazers of yesteryear.

A debt of gratitude is due to Judge Omar Platt, of Milford, for permission to use excerpts from *The History of Milford* (Tercentenary Edition).

M. R. W.

AUGUST 1949

xiv

Looking Backward

Built as a meeting house and high school in 1878, The Academy served as the Orange Town Hall until 1967 and as the Board of Education until 1989. It features stick-style elements and an elaborate gable screen facade. Photo by Peter J. Malia.

2

PART I

EARLY BEGINNING

AFTER crossing the Housatonic River, and riding north on the beautiful, new Wilbur Cross Parkway, the traveler is very soon notified "This is Orange." We would like to add a background of history to this peaceful scene of rolling hills and fertile meadows, so that the present generation may have a better understanding of the character and stamina of the pioneers who first cleared the way, making it easier for others to follow. Paraphrasing Daniel Webster's tribute to Dartmouth College in its early days, "She is a little town, nestled among the hills, but there are those who love her."

Though small in area and mileage, when compared with some of the other towns in the state, nevertheless it occupies a place of importance, since it is placed in a strategic point at the threshhold of a prominent city.

If Rome was founded on seven hills, so was Orange, and some of the names have come down from the Indians. Turkey Hill, Grassy or Grassie Hill, George's Cellar Hill, Indian Hill, Chestnut Ridge or Long Hill, Marsh Hill, and Cemetery Hill. Most of these hills are clearly indicated on the early maps of the town. In the days of unimproved roads, they were much more formidable than in the present state of graded, hard surfaced and easy slopes; excepting when King Winter coats them with ice. Then a liberal carpet of sand and extreme care are required to make the grades. Vastly different aspects are presented by the two main arteries that run through the town. The Derby Turnpike on the north is a four lane road of scenic beauty, passing placid lakes, crested hills, attractive homes, and culminating in the Wilbur Cross Parkway. In sharp contrast, the Milford Turnpike, or the Boston Post Road, on the south, is almost strictly commercial. A link of the four lane U. S. 1 highway, it is lined with shops, factories, business concerns of various kinds, taverns, restaurants, snack bars, service stations, and repair shops. It glows with Neon lights, and carries an almost continuous line of heavy trucking, twenty-four hours a day.

The history of the Town of Orange is indissolubly linked with that of the Town of Milford; for the first purchase from the Indians included all of the territory which comprised the town. When Charles I was King of England, there was increasing opposition to the requirements of the Crown and the Established Church of England, and the persecutions because of non-conformity to the tenets of the English Church. For this reason, increasing numbers of people were leaving their native shores to join the group who had started a colony in New England. A company on board the ship *Hector* left London in May 1637, under the leadership of Rev. John Davenport and Theophilus Eaton, of London, with Boston as their destination. A few weeks later, another group arrived in Boston, probably coming on the ship *Martin*. This group was under the leadership of Rev. Peter Prudden, who came from Hertfordshire. Among the original settlers of Milford, the following members were known to have come from Hertfordshire: Edmund Tapp, James Prudden, William Fowler, Thomas and Hannah Buckingham, Thomas Welch, Richard Platt, Henry Stonehill, and William East.

Having reached the Massachusetts Bay Colony, the new arrivals remained in the vicinity of Boston for nearly a year, and were strongly urged to make their permanent home there. But John Davenport and Peter Prudden had other plans, and wanted to establish a colony of their own.

In August, 1637, a group from the Davenport colony, headed by Theophilus Eaton, came down to the region of the Quinnipiac River in Connecticut, to investigate a report made by some scouts who had been pursuing the Pequot tribe of Indians. They were so favorably impressed with the contour of the land that they wanted to hold

4

this land for the rest of their friends. Accordingly, they left a group of seven to remain throughout the winter, to be sure of possession.

In April, 1638, the two groups, headed by Davenport and Prudden, sailed from Boston, headed for the Quinnipiac region. The Davenport group formed the New Haven Colony, and the Prudden contingent remained with them for over a year. A separate allotment, known as the Hertfordshire section, was granted to them. They cleared the land, planted crops, and built houses. During the summer of 1638, very soon after reaching New Haven, Rev. Mr. Prudden went to the town of Wethersfield to serve as preacher. He was a forceful man and won the devotion of his listeners, who wanted to join him in founding a new settlement, having him as its pastor. Thomas Tapping, Robert Treat, John Sherman, Thomas Tibbals. John Fletcher, George Hubbard, Richard Miles, and Andrew Benton came down from Wethersfield with him to join the Hertfordshire group in founding the Milford Colony.

In 1637, Sergeant Thomas Tibbals had been out on a scouting trip and was very favorably impressed by the looks of the land near the mouth of the river which the Indians called Wepowage. He thought it would be an excellent place for a settlement, and recommended it to the Prudden party. Accordingly, on February 12, 1639, with Serg. Tibbals as their guide, Edmund Tapp, William Fowler, Benjamin Fenn, Zachariah Whitman, and Alexander Bryan made a trip to the Wepawaug and purchased the land from Ansantawae, a sachem of the Paugusset Indians who had a village on the banks of the river. The purchase price was "six coats, ten blankets, one kettle, twelve hatchets, twelve hoes, two dozen knives and a dozen small mirrors." In his History of Connecticut (1797) Dr. Benjamin Trumbull says, "They first purchased of the Indians all the tract which lies between New Haven and Stratford river, and between the Sound on the south, and a stream called Two Mile Brook on the

5

north which is the boundary line between Milford and Derby."

Two Mile Brook is located in the western part of Orange, and is the boundary line between Orange and Derby. This first purchase, therefore, included nearly all of the present towns of Orange and Milford, and part of the Towns of Woodbridge and West Haven.

According to the History of Milford, the deeding of land to its new owners was consummated by the old English "twig and turf" ceremony. After both parties had signed the deed, Ansantawae was handed a piece of turf and a twig; taking the piece of turf in one hand, and the twig in the other, he thrust the twig into the turf, and handed it to the settlers, thus showing that the Indians relinquished all the land specified in the deed, and everything growing upon it. It was said that the Paugusset Indians made this sale, hoping that they would obtain help from the Colonists against their constant foe, the Mohawks, who continually were making raids on them. It took several months of preparation before the settlers were ready to take possession of their property.

On the morning of August 22, 1639, the Davenport group had met in council in Robert Newman's barn, on Grove St., New Haven, and formed the First Church of New Haven. In the afternoon of the same day, the Hertfordshire group met in the same barn and formed the First Church of Milford. Both churches chose "Seven Pillars" as the governing body of the church. This was according to the Scripture, "Wisdom hath builded her house, she hath hewn out her seven pillars." The "Seven Pillars" of the Milford church were Peter Prudden, Zachariah Whitman, William Fowler, John Astwood, Edmund Tapp, Thomas Welch, and Thomas Buckingham. Having purchased their land and organized their church, they were now ready to go and possess their land.

In his "History of the Colony of New Haven," Lambert describes the journey, "The body of planters moved from New Haven by land, following the devious Indian foot-path, driving their cattle and other domestic animals

6

before them, while their household and farming utensils, and the materials for the common house, were taken round by water. Serg. Thomas Tibbals piloted the company through the woods to the place, he having been there a number of times before." The route followed is supposed to have crossed the West River up near Westville, followed through what is now Forest Road to Allingtown, thence down through Campbell Avenue to Main Street, West Haven; then west over Bonny Hill and Prindle Hill, to Marsh Hill and on to Milford.

All safely arrived, the planters erected their common house at the head of the harbor, on the west side, and a few rude huts, for temporary residence.

From the early records we quote the following: "The first general court (or town meeting) of the planters was held on the 20th of November, 1639. It was then agreed and determined that the power of electing officers and persons to divide the land and manage the interests of the plantation should be in the church, only. It was also agreed and determined that all the business of the plantation in their meetings and by their magistrates and officers should be done according to the written word of God, as each one should have light and knowledge therein." Thus was the Bible made their code of laws for the present. The persons chosen at this first meeting for "Judges in all civil affairs and to try all causes between man and man, to punish offences and sin against the Commandments were, William Fowler, Esq., Edmund Tapp, Esq., Deacon Zachariah Whitman, Captain John Atwood, and Richard Miles."

They were ordered to "hold a court once in every six weeks, and invested with discretionary power to call a general meeting and to promote the general good."

At this first town meeting there was much discussion as to whether or not voting and office-holding should be confined to church members. This was finally passed in the affirmative, and the right of franchise as "free planters" was accordingly granted to forty-four church members. Following is the list taken from the town records.

7

Zachariah Whitman
Thomas Welsh
Thomas Wheeler
Edmund Tapp
Thomas Buckingham
Richard Miles
Richard Platt
Thomas Topping
Mr. Peter Prudden
William Fowler
John Astwood
Richard Baldwin
Benjamin Fenn
Samuel Coley
John Peacocke

Henry Stonehill
Nathaniel Baldwin
James Prudden
Thomas Baker
George Clark, Sr.
George Hubbard
Jasper Gunn
John Fletcher
Alexander Bryan
Francis Bolt
Micah Tomkins
John Birdsey
Edmund Harvey
John Lane
William East

Thomas Lawrence
Thomas Sanford
Timothy Baldwin
George Clark, Jr.
John Burwell
Henry Botsford
Joseph Baldwin
Philip Hatly
Nicholas Camp
John Rogers
Thomas Uffott
Nathaniel Briscoe
Thomas Tibbals
John Sherman

The following persons are recorded immediately after, but not as free-planters:

Robert Plum
Roger Terrell
Joseph Northrup

John Baldwin
William Slough
Andrew Benton

William Brookes
Robert Treat
Henry Lyon

In his "History of Connecticut," Hollister says, "A more substantial company of emigrants never followed a clergyman into the wild woods of America than the fathers of Milford."

Within the palisades which were set up, there were two residential streets, which extended on either side of the Wepawaug River and West End Brook. Sixty-five home lots were laid out, averaging three acres each. Mr. Prudden was assigned twice this amount, about seven acres.

Each man paid his share of the expense of the purchase and settlement of the plantation. All divisions of land were made in exact proportion to the sum paid by each planter. To each planter, a home or building lot was first laid out in the center of the town; and then an equal proportion of land and meadow elsewhere was allotted to him, according to the number of persons in his family. Every child had a division. The place where each man should have his division and proportion of ground was usually determined by casting lots. Rev. Mr. Prudden was reputed to have been a man of wealth when he left

8

England; also, his wife had quite an estate in her own right.

The northern section of the town was not surveyed until about 1687, and very little building was undertaken before 1700. Richard Bryan, son of Alexander Bryan, one of the original planters, owned the largest amount of land; so this district was first called "Bryan's Farms," and later was known as North Milford.

INDIANS

The Paugussetts who lived on the west side of the Housatonic, and the Wepawaugs who lived on the east bank, were the same tribe of people. The territory of this clan stretched fifteen or eighteen miles along the coast, and comprised nearly the present townships of Monroe, Huntington, Trumbull, Bridgeport, Stratford, Milford, Orange, and Derby.

They lived chiefly on shell food; oysters and clams. Large heaps of oyster shells are evidence of this fact. Besides using clams for food, they found another use for them. In the round clam or quahaug, about half an inch of the inside of some of the shells is of a purple color. This the Indians broke off and converted into beads, named by them "scuhauhock" or black money. This was said to be of twice the value of their wampum, or white money, made from periwinkle, and called "metauhock."

In his book, "Statistical Account, Town of Milford," Rev. Erastus Scranton says, "In this town were great numbers of Indians. They had four considerable settlements; in the center of the town, another one at the Point, another at Turkey Hill, in the northwest part of the town, and another about one quarter of a mile north of Washington Bridge. At Turkey Hill, they had a fort, with flankers, also they had a burying ground at Turkey Hill, on the banks of the Housatonic River, about sixty rods north of Turkey Hill brook, and fifty rods south of Two Mile brook, which is now the boundary line between Milford and Derby. There they buried great numbers of their

9

dead, and made doleful lamentations and howlings at the time of interment. The last Indian interred here was Betty Taukus, aged 63, on June 4, 1794. The ground where this burying place was, at present is occupied for the purpose of husbandry. There are but fifteen graves which have any monuments remaining."

After a lapse of some years, the Indians complained that they had sold all their land and had no place to live, so they asked the town to assign them some place on the river, where they might live and fish and hunt. Accordingly, about a hundred acres of land at Turkey Hill were reserved for their use and benefit. Tradition has it that Turkey Hill received its name because wild turkeys were numerous there, and used to fly across the Housatonic River at that point. The original Turkey Hill is the steep hill that rises from the Housatonic River, opposite Two Mile Island.

About 1665, the Chief Ansantawae, with most of his tribe, moved to Turkey Hill, where he soon died. But some of the tribe continued to live there for over a hundred years. The last family of the tribe was named Hatchett. Molly Hatchett was the wife, according to Indian custom, of John Hatchett, and they had four children. He died at an early age, so she was a widow for many years. Molly Hatchett was a very tall and powerful woman, with piercing black eyes, and long, black hair, falling over her shoulders. She always wore a white blanket shawl, a man's hat, and carried a cane or a hatchet. Like most of the Indians, she was a basket maker. She had the custom of making basket rattles, holding six kernels of corn, which she presented to any new born baby. However, if there happened to be more than six children in the family, she added the corresponding number of kernels. Her family moved to Kent, to join the Scatacook tribe, but she lived in a little house, all alone, and was very much respected in the neighborhood. Her real name is unknown, but she was often called "Magawiska." Her great failing was a fondness for "uncupe" as she called rum. She died January 17, 1829, almost one hundred years old.

10

In 1671, the Wepawaug fort of the Indians, which
had escaped the attack of the Mohawks in 1648, was set
on fire in the middle of the night by eleven young men
from the settler's colony. Their motives were unknown;
but it is probable that, like many lads of these less staid
and sober days, they had a more acute appreciation of fun
than of justice. The Indians complained, and the culprits
being discovered, they were sentenced by the General
Court of New Haven County, to pay a fine of ten pounds
each. The Indians were appeased, and afterwards rebuilt
their fort. However, they appealed to the settlers for protection. A committee, composed of Ephraim Strong, Esq.,
Joseph Woodruff, Esq., and Colonel Benjamin Fenn, was
appointed to look after the land which had been allotted
to the Indians, and see that it was not encroached upon
by outsiders. This committee was "to prosecute in due
form any person who had or shall cut timber or wood,
or carry off any timber, or should fence in any of said
land, or any way trespass upon it."

The man who acquired the land where the old burying ground was treated it with great respect, and would
never allow a plow to disturb the rude grave markers.
Some said that medical students from Yale did not have
as deep a degree of sentiment. When the railroad between
New Haven and Derby was built, about 1870, in the cut
near what was known as "Tynan's Crossing," they went
right through the old Indian cemetery. The bones and
relics which were unearthed were sent to the Indian
museum in upper New York City. Even to the present
day, arrow-heads, bones, and relics have been found near
the Wepawaug River, or at Turkey Hill. At the top of the
ledge in the section of the old New Haven and Derby
railroad, known as the Turkey Hill cut, there was found
an old Indian mortar and pounding stone, where the
Indians pounded their corn.

The families who lived in the Indian Hill section, on
Chestnut Ridge, belonged to the Scatacook tribe, who
settled in the town of Kent. Their chief was Gideon Wau-
wehu. A son of Gideon lived in Seymour, as the chief of

the tribe there. The tribe at Kent flourished for many years, and was well thought of by the people of that region. Barber says of them, "During the Revolutionary War this tribe furnished one hundred warriors. It is said they were able to communicate intelligence from the sea-coast to Stockbridge, Mass. a distance of a hundred miles, in two hours. This was accomplished by means of Indian yells or whoops, from their men who were stationed at proper places along the borders of the Housatonic River."

About 1776, it is believed that members of the Scata-cook tribe moved from Kent down to the Orange district, and lived there the rest of their lives. Their burial place on Indian Hill, north of the Derby Turnpike, and about three and one-half miles west of the center of New Haven, in a direct line, is now hidden by a growth of forestry. These grounds may be found about thirty rods northeast from the first turn in the Indian Hill road, going north from Long Hill, or Chestnut Ridge. Most of the graves may be found in the westerly end of a rectangular enclosure. It is now the property of the New Haven Water Co. These Indians were basket makers, and the handiwork of "Aunt Icy" was well known. She was the wife of Brien Oviatt, and lived to be one hundred and two years old. She and her children were highly esteemed by her neighbors, who gathered to celebrate her one hundredth birthday in 1900. She remembered the last two Indians who were buried in the family plot on the hill-side. Her own family, however, are buried in the Ever-green Cemetery in New Haven. Aunt Icy's daughter Polly first married a man named Brown. They had two sons, Frank and Augustus. Gus Brown was the headwaiter at the old New Haven House for some years. Later Polly married a colored man named Jackson. Polly Jackson had the reputation of being a fine cook. It was said that no one attempted a wedding or a large party without having Polly make the cake, which was her specialty.

The ordinary sugar used by housekeepers at this time was called C sugar, a light brown and coarser variety than our regular granulated sugar. The story is told that some-

Key to 100th birthday picture, *left to right*, *standing*: Mrs. Dora Shillinglaw, Frank Peck, Minnie Clark, Theron Alling, Henry Oviatt, John Oviatt, a grandson, William Russell, Dwight Alling, Elizur Russell.
Seated: Mrs. Fields Andrew, little Fields, Elias Clark, Edith Edmundson, Billy Sharpe (grandson), Mrs. Sharpe, Mrs. Brien Oviatt (Aunt Icy), Polly Jackson, Mrs. William Russell, Mrs. Elizur Russell, Mrs. Dwight Alling, Mrs. Wade, Mrs. Luke Clark.
On the ground: Mrs. Leonard Andrew, Beulah Russell, Ruby Russell, Inez Russell, Lottie Peck.

one had engaged Polly to make the cake for a party. The man of the house thought he would be especially helpful, so brought home granulated sugar; but Polly pushed it aside disdainfully. "You get me C sugar if you want me to make your cake; I won't touch that fancy kind."

Sue Fanchus was one of the Indians who used to wander around the town. Some charitable woman made her a present of a blanket as a needed protection against the winter's cold. Whereupon Sue cut a circular hole in the center and passed her head through the opening; and thus by a single stroke of genius, converted it into a convenient article of wearing apparel.

One of the last survivors of the Indians was Elizabeth Roberts, who was a mixture of Indian and African blood. She had the nomad instinct of the Indian and could not be depended on to stay very long in one place. She was a very good worker when the spirit moved her to be industrious.

Mr. Scranton says, "As far as I am acquainted, the causes of their diminution are debility arising from idleness, general and excessive use of spirituous liquors by both males and females, and scanty or irregular diet. Many of them died of a pulmonary consumption."

The Milford Indians were considered for the most part as friendly to their white neighbors. Although there is no record of any bodily injury or any great property damage having been done by the Indians, still there was always that fear; and for the first fifty years, the settlers lived within the protection of the palisades. The men would go out to their out-lying property to work in the fields during the daytime, returning to their homes and the shelter of the palisades at night.

That the Indians roamed up and down the Wepawaug River is very plainly indicated by the hundreds of arrow-heads, scrapers, tomahawks, or other utensils found along its banks. Near the place where the Race Brook joins the Wepawaug would seem to have been a favorite spot for camp-fires or pow-wows, because of the great quantities of specimens unearthed there. In the "Song of

Hiawatha," the old arrow-maker "made his arrow-heads of chalcedony, flint and jasper, smoothed and sharpened at the edges, hard and polished."

That exactly describes the varieties which have been found in that locality by the Czenkus family, who live next door to the Cedar Crest Recreation Camp. Some of their specimens have been placed in the Peabody Museum at Yale University. Howard B. Treat has also a remarkable collection, found in the same section. Carleton V. Woodruff has some choice specimens, found in the Turkey Hill section.

The old Indian burying ground in Turkey Hill was abandoned years ago, but at the present time there is a burial place very near the old location. It is the Hebrew Cemetery of Ansonia and Derby.

FIRST SETTLERS

As has been stated, Alexander Bryan, one of the original Milford "Planters," was probably the first to own any considerable amount of land in the town, hence the name of "Bryan's Farms." If all of the historians are correct, the holdings of the Bryan family were so extensive that no wonder the section was named for them. One authority states, "John Bryan lived south of the Green, and his son Richard had a store on the east side."[2] According to the records, Samuel Treat married Frances Bryan, daughter of Richard and Mary Pantry Bryan, of Grassy Hill. A house still stands on what was the property of Alexander Bryan, which is thought to be the first house in the town. It stands on the north side of Old Tavern Road, with the land extending to the westerly line of Lambert Road. This house is now occupied by Miss Virginia Nye Rhodes.[3] Alexander Bryan was one of the Trustees of the first Milford Purchase. At his death, his farm of three hundred acres passed to his son, Richard. On November 20, 1720, Richard Bryan conveyed to his son Richard "208 acres at High Plains, with dwellings,

15

etc., where he now lives, bounded on all sides by the high-way." So it looks as if the house was built in the fall of 1720.

The story is that during the erection of the house, the Indians watched so attentively that a guard was set to watch them. On March 26, 1707, John Rogers deeded Joseph Rogers fifty acres at High Plains, and again on March 15, 1717, twelve more acres in the same locality, namely the plain extending south from the Orange church, on the westerly side of the highway.

How many dwellings were erected in the southern part of what is now Orange in the early years of the eighteenth century does not definitely appear, but it would seem that the number must have been considerable, as indicated by the vote of the Town of Milford in 1750, referred to by Mr. Barber, "that money be appropriated to set up a school at Bryan's Farms, it being populated enough that one is deemed necessary."

In a Town Meeting, April 25, 1721, a committee was appointed to lay out the present Oggs Meadow Road. As reported by this committee, this layout began on the "north line of the 'First Purchase'" and extended south-erly on the western side of the Wepawaug River to a point where the Derby Turnpike is now located, and turned eastward to join a road that came down from the Race, between the 2nd and 3rd Shots. (Just what was meant by the Shots is hard to tell. One old meaning of a shot was a corner or plot of land.) However, need of a formally laid-out highway indicates that there were dwellings on or near it.

The early settlers brought the English system of cur-rency with them and used it for many years before they adopted our more simple decimal system.

A page from the account book of one of the early citizens gives an idea of how some elderly woman was cared for, until her career was ended:

Jan. 15, 1757 Mother, Dr. to 1 pair shoes   0 - 05 - 0
        also to 12 pounds of flax @ 5½   0 - 05 - 6

Anno.	1756	Mother Beard, Dr. to her board, 7 weeks	1 - 15 - 0
Dec.	1756	Paid Bro. Hull, on Mother's account	3 - 14 - 0
		also to going to Derby for her	0 - 02 - 6
Anno.	1757	Mother Beard, Dr. for her board, 6 weeks	1 - 10 - 0
		also for carrying her to Derby	0 - 03 - 6
Jan. 18,	1758	Mother, Dr. to 2 pounds, 16s. and 1 penny	2 - 16 - 1
		also to 10 pounds of flax at 9d.	0 - 07 - 6
Aug.	1758	to 40 shillings and 10d. money	2 - 00 - 10
		also 11 shillings to Dr. Canfield	0 - 11 - 0
		also to 1 ounce of metridate	0 - 01 - 0
Jan.	1759	Mother Beard, Dr. to cambrick & holland	
		for 2 caps, and making them	0 - 04 - 0
Feb.	1760	paid to Bro. Hull, six pounds, three shillings	
		for keeping mother	6 - 03 - 0
Anno.	1760	Mother, Dr. for board, 4 months & 3 weeks	5 - 18 - 0
Nov.	1760	paid Bro. Hull, for keeping Mother	2 - 01 - 4
Funeral			
Charges		to eighteen pair of gloves at 2/6 *	2 - 05 - 0
		to ten yards of hat crape at 2/6 *	1 - 05 - 0
		to 3 hundred of nails at 1/ 9	0 - 01 - 9
		to 1 pr. dove tails for the coffin	0 - 06 - 0
		for the coffin	0 - 14 - 0
		for digging the grave	0 - 10 - 0
		for tolling the passing bell	0 - 03 - 0

* Probably the gloves & hat crape were for the mourners.

FORMATION OF THE CHURCH

The history of the town could not be written without first considering the church, for that was the heart of the community. Besides being used for divine services it was the only auditorium available; the Town Meetings were held there, as well as any court or trial. For nearly a hundred years the hardy settlers, sons of the early colonists for the most part, had made their way on Sunday to one or the other meeting houses in the southern part of the town. This was truly a hardship, especially in winter; for the distance was long, the roads unimproved, and the principal method for the whole family was walking. Then, in winter, after suffering the discomforts of the journey, the church-goers had to enter a cold meeting

THE ORIGINAL CHURCH WITH THE HORSE-SHEDS

house, and must spend the day there, sitting through its two long services.

Late in the afternoon there was the return trip, back to a cold hearth, and after doing the nightly chores, to retire to cold sleeping rooms, and plunge into icy sheets, perchance offering up a prayer of thanksgiving that Sunday came but once a week.

By official order, every one was obliged to attend church.*

Feeling the necessity of having divine service a little nearer their homes, in 1792 they erected a simple and modest meeting house, 36 by 30 feet, about two and a half rods south of the present church.

Then they petitioned the Societies of the two churches in Milford for preaching at Bryan's Farms in winter. That year they were granted six Sundays, with the minister riding up from Milford on horseback to conduct the services. The clergymen of the two Milford churches alternated in conducting these services. The next year they had ten services, and in 1796 the number was increased to twelve.

But twelve services during the winter did not satisfy the early fathers. They wanted divine worship made available every Sabbath. So they presented the following petition to the General Assembly in 1804:

"To the Honorable the General Assembly of the State of Connecticut to be holden at Hartford in and for said state on the second Tuesday in May, A.D. 1804.

"The petition of Samuel Treat of the first Ecclesiastical society and Joseph Treat of the second Ecclesiastical society in the Town of Milford, in the county of New Haven, and others belonging to each of said societies, their neighbors and Associates, all living in the part of said two societies commonly called Bryan's Farms humbly sheweth:— That they are deeply impressed with the importance of a constant attendance for themselves and families on public worship, and while their attendance is always accompanied with inconvenience, it is sometimes

* "Be it enacted by the Governor, Council and Representatives in General Court assembled, and by the Authority of the same that: All and every person and persons whatsoever, shall and they are hereby required on the Lord's Day, carefully to apply themselves to the duties of religion and piety, publically and privately; and that whatsoever person shall not duly attend the public worship of God on the Lord's Day, in some congregation by law allowed, unless hindered by sickness, or otherwise detained or hindered, shall incur the penalty of three shillings for every offense, and being presented by authority for such neglect, shall be deemed guilty thereof, if such person shall not be able to prove to the satisfaction of said authority that he or she has attended the said worship."

rendered impossible. That some of the petitioners live at a distance of seven miles, and a medium of their travel will exceed four miles, to the present Meeting Houses. That they are fully persuaded that the number of Inhabitants, the wealth and respectability of the Town of Milford, will warrant the establishment of a separate Society in the Northerly part of said Town. That the inhabitants in the part are united in the object and feel it their duty to petition for the establishment of such a Society.

"That the Limits for which they pray will comprehend about one-third part of the Grand List of the said Town, and about one-third part of the Land and will be in a compact form. That said Societies are each of them possessed of large funds for the support of the ministry and public worship.

"Your petitioners, therefore, in behalf of themselves and their associates, pray your Honors to incorporate them into a new Ecclesiastical Society, with all the forms, privileges and immunities, usually granted or appertaining to other Ecclesiastical Societies in this State, and that the Lines and Limits of said new Society be as follows viz: Beginning at the Line between New Haven and Milford, 35 rods north of the head of Oyster creek or Oyster River; thence in a westerly direction to the place where two roads intersect, about 12 rods south of John Treat's house; thence to the stone bridge on the Derby road over Weaver's Brook; thence to Housatonic river at the north end of the upper meadow, thence on said river to the Derby line, thence on Derby line till the same is intersected by Woodbridge line, thence on the line between Milford and Woodbridge to Hog Meadow road, thence northerly in said Road to the southwest corner of Enoch Baldwin's land, thence southerly about six rods to the northwest corner of Richard Baldwin's land, thence easterly on the North Line of his Land to an Highway, thence southerly in said Highway to the Southwest corner of Nathaniel Camp's Land, thence easterly on the Southerly Line of said Camp's Land to

21

the ancient Line to the place of the beginning, and that all the Inhabitants living within said limits be comprehended in said Society. And your petitioners Further pray that they may have asserted and set out to them for the support of the ministry and public worship among them, their part and proportion of the said funds of each of the said Societies, according to their Grand List as taken from each of said Societies, or in some way grant their relief, and they as in duty bound will ever pray.

Samuel Treat (for themselves and associates)

Joseph Treat	Benjamin Fenn, Jr.	Ephraim N. Lambert
Samuel Fenn	Jonathan Treat	Joel Woodruff
Elias Clark	Benjamin Clark, Jr.	John Treat
Isaac Treat	Joseph Pardee	Jeremiah Parker
Samuel Treat	Asa Sperry	Margaret Andrew
Robert Treat, Jr.	Asa Platt	Isaac Nettleton
Amos Mallory	Jonah Treat	Andrew Parker
David Treat	Joseph Stone	Robert Treat
David Nettleton	Benjamin Clark	David Treat, Jr.
Amos Nettleton	Mary Woodruff	Enoch Clark, Jr.
Josiah Fowler	Elias Andrew	Jonathan Fowler
Ichabod A. Woodruff	Josiah Boardman	Joseph Treat
Samuel Fenn, Jr.	William Fowler	Hezekiah Lounsbury
Joseph Treat, Jr.	David Johnson	Richard Treat
Aaron Hine	Jonas Boughton	Abraham Hine"
Peck Fenn	Jesse Hodge	52
Gideon Alling	Elias Clark, Jr.	
Aaron Hine, Jr.	John Lambert	

A former petition had been denied owing to the earnest opposition of the southern part of the town. But this time the request was allowed, a charter was granted, the Society was organized on the first Monday in December, 1804. And for over a hundred years, the Society held its annual meeting on that date.

Regular preaching services began immediately after the organization of the Society, and on February 24, Mr. Erastus Scranton, a student at Yale, a candidate for the ministry, preached his first sermon and continued to occupy the pulpit until July when, after his graduation, he was ordained pastor of the church and society. He was a native of Madison and was described as a "strong, tall,

22

farmer looking man." It is related that when his father was asked what Erastus was doing, he replied, "He is preaching the everlasting Gospel to the heathen of North Milford." The church was organized March 13, 1805, with a membership of fifty-four, all of whom had been dismissed by letter from the two Milford churches for this purpose.

Right here it must be stated that there was a great distinction in the use of the words. The church was the body of Christian believers, the building in which they met to worship was called the Meeting House. A witness to this fact is the road leading west from the Green, which has always been called "Meeting-house Lane." At the same time a plot north of the church was set aside for use as a burial ground, or "God's-acre," and the first person to be buried there was Joseph, the young son of Joseph and Eunice Treat, on November 2, 1805.

From the records of the Church or the Ecclesiastical Society can be gained much information of those early days. On December 7, 1807, it was voted that a tax of four cents and five mills be laid upon the Dollar upon the polls and rateable estate of the inhabitants of North Milford Society for the purpose of supporting the Gospel and defraying the necessary charges of said Society, and that Benjamin Fenn be appointed Collector of above tax. Also voted "that Benjamin Fenn set monuments of stone in the burying-ground, so as to make the lots conspicuous."

At the annual meeting of the Ecclesiastical Society held December 4, 1809, it was voted to build a suitable building for public worship. Voted "that the meeting house stand on the corner of Mr. Samuel Treat's lot, which he had donated for the purpose, and about two and a half rods north of the present meeting house."

Also it was voted that for the purpose of building said house, two thousand dollars be raised by subscription. Also, "that no person who subscribes shall be bound to pay what he subscribes unless the sum of at least two thousand dollars be raised." Benjamin Fenn, David Treat,

Samuel Treat, David Nettleton, and John Bryan were appointed a committee "to make enquiry and to report of what materials, of what dimensions and in what manner will be best to build said house." Mr. Samuel Treat offered to give the Society land enough to set the house upon, provided that it was put on the corner of his lot, and take no more of his land.

At a Society's meeting, held on December 18, 1808,[4] it was voted to accept the above offer, and that the surplus money in the Treasury which arose from the tax on the list of 1808 be paid over to Mr. Samuel Treat for land to be leveled for a Green.

It was voted that the "house be fifty feet in length and forty feet in width, also that there be a steeple built with the house. Also, that the house be arched, and that the pulpit be built at one end of the house, and the door or doors at the other. Also that the steeple be built in the most fashionable style." There was much discussion as to the material, whether it should be of brick or wood. It was finally voted to build of wood. The building committee was empowered to buy the timber needed to complete the building after procuring all they could by donation.

The building was raised on the 25th, 26th, 27th, and 28th days of June, 1810. That it took four days is not surprising to one who has seen the timbers that went into the frame. The posts are of oak, ten inches square, and so perfectly hewed that they look as if they had been planed. Even the ridge-pole is seven inches square, and the other timbers are proportional in size and equally perfect in finish.

David Hoadley, the architect, who was famous for his churches, drew the plans for the building. His bill of $825.00 was the largest item on the total cost of the structure.

An amusing anecdote has come down through the years concerning the ridge-pole. The building committee canvassed the town to find the right kind of tree, which stood straight and true for over a hundred feet before it branched out, and which was large enough to cut a piece of timber, seven inches square, when completed. Such a tree was found down on the southern line of the town, on the farm of Isaac Treat. (There were two or three Isaac Treats in the town.) This Mr. Treat was not of the church group; but the committee asked him to give it, just the same.

In Yankee fashion, he replied that he would give the tree provided that Colonel Potter would cut off his queue. The Colonel was the last man in town to retain the Colonial style of wearing the hair. He was not so enthusiastic over the church, either, so Mr. Treat believed he was safe in his offer. Possibly the Colonel was just waiting for a good excuse; anyway, he was a good sport and went and had his hair cut; whereupon Mr. Treat donated the much-wanted tree.

It took some months to complete the building, and evidentally they planned as the work progressed; for at a society meeting held on October 1, 1810, it was "voted that the house be finished with pews, also that they have banisters next the alleys. That the front seat of the gallery be built in the form of a semi-circle, and that the windows be secured by springs." The house was dedicated on April 17, 1811, the Rev. Bazaleel Pinneo, of the First Church in Milford, preaching the sermon.

The church bell has always played an important part in the life of the town. It summoned people to church on Sunday; it served as a fire alarm; it was tolled to announce the death of anyone in the town. The signal was nine strokes for a man, seven for a woman, five for a boy and three for a girl. This was repeated, and then the age was solemnly tolled off. On the day of the funeral, when the procession approached the cemetery, the "passing bell" was slowly tolled until everyone had reached the grave of the deceased. With no telephones, thus was the news announced to the town.

The epitaph on the headstone of Samuel Prudden, who

died July 12, 1819, aged 78, and who lies in the Orange cemetery, bears out these statements:

> "Oft as the bell with solemn toll
> Speaks the departure of a soul,
> Let each one ask himself, Am I
> Prepared should I be called to die?"

Another use was found for the church bell, for on December 7, 1818, it was voted "that Jonathan Judd be sexton to ring the bell on the Sabbath, on Lecture days, and every night at nine o'clock, Saturday night excepted, for $20.00 a year."

Evidently the first bell they procured proved defective, for at the annual Society meeting, held in December, 1822, they first appointed a committee to see what could be done to have the bell mended, but on further discussion, it was voted that if fifty dollars could be raised by subscription, the Society would take from the Treasury the remainder of the amount necessary to get a new bell. This was done, and with great difficulty a new bell was installed in the belfry.

The church stands on high ground, and the top of the steeple is visible from almost any part of the town. The seating arrangement was much different than at the present time. The seats on the main floor were reserved for the middle-aged people. All the youth, the unmarried young men and women, and generally the younger married couples, were seated in the high galleries. There seemed some controversy as to which seats certain persons should occupy, and at the Ecclesiastical Society meeting, December 7, 1818, it was voted "that all widows be seated as when their husbands were living." It was further voted that "the house should be seated according to list and age, and every person shall send his age to the Seaters." That vote did not meet with very popular response, for at the very next meeting of the society it was voted "that this society pay no attention to what the Seating committee have done, in seating the house, but go back to their old pews."

Although they had no organ, they had a choir. The tune was pitched by a tuning fork, and the voices were accompanied by a violin and a bass-viol. Singing was considered important, and at a meeting held December 1, 1817, it was voted that "fifty dollars be expended for the use of reviving and teaching singing, and that Samuel Buckingham, Alpheus Clark, Enoch R. Platt and Edmund R. Fowler be a committee to procure a teacher and set up said school and furnish all necessaries, and see that the same is paid for." The singing school was held in the Academy.

In 1804, a public library was established, which by 1816 had increased to 144 volumes, mostly on religious subjects, which is an index of the character of the citizens: they were sober, intelligent, and industrious. The choice of books obtainable for a library at that time was very limited, as religious books predominated.

From Timothy Dwight's "Journeys in New England," September 17, 1811: "After passing the western boundary of the township of New Haven, we entered the parish of North Milford. The surface of this parish is formed of easy undulations. The soil is rich and the inhabitants are industrious, sober, frugal and virtuous. The state of Connecticut is distinguished, perhaps from all other countries by a commanding regard to personal character.

'Here, in truth,
Not in pretense, man is esteemed as man
Not here how rich, of what peculiar blood,
Or office high; but of what genuine worth
What talents bright and useful, what good deeds,
What piety to God, what love to man
The question is. To this an answer fair
The general heart secures.'

"The people of North Milford, plain as they are, have built one of the handsomest churches in the county of New Haven; and have thus shown that they have a taste for the beautiful as well as a proper attachment to

27

the useful. The parish consists chiefly of plantations. The road from New Haven to Derby is excellent, and having been recently laid out through unoccupied grounds, is in a great measure solitary. Planters, however, are already multiplying upon it, and within a short time it will be lined with houses."

There were three different purchases of land from the Indians at various times; the first purchase on February 12, 1639, included all of the territory comprising the present town of Orange, and extended as far north as what was known as the "old path," which was a road from the district known as Derby to New Haven. This old path as it entered Derby was very steep, and naturally, after the construction of the Derby Turnpike, was little used.

ORANGE SECTIONAL NAMES

In the early days of the town, the territory was designated by sections or districts. The section in the northwest part, running into Woodbridge from the region where the Derby Turnpike now runs, was called Oggs Meadow. The northeasterly and easterly sections were called Dogburn. The tradition in regard to this name is that the Indians, during one of their pow-wows, became so excited that they cast a dog into the fire and burned him. The southeasterly section was called Scotland. The section running south from the Orange Green on the east side of the highway was called High Plains. The section lying west of High Plains was called Town Plain. The section extending from Milford, and over and adjoining the road from Milford to Bethany, was called the Race. The section between the Race and the Dogburn section was called White Plain. The section extending southerly from the Derby Turnpike region was called Grassie or Grassy Hill; and the section west of this, and extending to the Housatonic River, was called Turkey Hill. A section in the extreme northwest and extending into Derby was called Sodom; and, lastly, the section lying west of the Derby to Milford road was called George's Cellar Hill. Despite much investigation, the origin of the name Race is still unknown. One tradition is that farmers living in Milford, and owning land up through Bethany, were accustomed to go to their land in companies and on horseback. Some of the younger men were believed to have tried out their horses that way. But the fact that many of the deeds which describe land as located "at the Race" refer to tracts located a considerable distance from the road, indicates that the origin of the name Race (or Homes Race, or Holmes, his Race, as it was promiscuously called) has no definite explanation.

In the writings of Silas J. Peck of Woodbridge, the following item is found: "Seventeen years before the settlement was made in New Haven (about 1620), the Dutch took formal possession of all the land from New York, or New Amsterdam, as they called it, and set up a trading post and fort at or near Milford. Holmes is a distinctly Dutch name, and I believe that some seafaring men of that nationality sailed up the shore to Milford, probably on a voyage of discovery. If they landed, as they must have done, they saw that the land was good, and decided they would acquire a portion of it for themselves. I can plainly see them asking the Captain for shore leave. The consent was finally given, on the condition that all who went were to travel as far north as they could go in a given time, and the one that went the farthest was to have all the land he covered. Holmes must have had the greater advantage, and when he had made the allotted time, he found himself at that place a good half mile beyond what is now the Bethany line, at a natural fortification, a pile of rocks that had the appearance of a fort. It is in fact a place where one man could hold off an indefinite number of enemies, and, since the dim past has been known as Holmes, his fort."

Notes

1. Woodruff noted that the Scatacook tribe moved to the Orange district in 1776. At the time, the area was still known as North Milford. Orange was not founded until 1822, 46 years later.

2. Richard Bryan's store was located on the west side of the Green, not the east side as Miss Woodruff noted.

3. In 1949 this house was still standing on Orange Center Road across from Martin Lane, but it was soon after taken down. The house at 131 Old Tavern Road, once owned by Miss Virginia Nye Rhoades, is said to have been built by Nathan Bryan, ca. 1750. It is still standing and restored as the Nathan Bryan-William Andrew House by The Orange Historical Society.

4. The Ecclesiastical Society meeting that voted to accept Samuel Treat's land offer for the Congregational Church was held on December 18, 1809, not 1808, as Woodruff mentioned.

The Town Gets A New Name

PART II.

FORMATION OF THE TOWN OF ORANGE

THE western part of the New Haven Colony was known as West Farms, or West Haven. As the years went by, the inhabitants of this section were not entirely satisfied, claiming that they had to pay their share of the expenses and improvements of New Haven, but received a small amount for their own improvements.

Feeling that they were strong enough for self government, they petitioned the General Assembly to be set aside as a separate town in 1785 and again in 1787. On both occasions, they were vigorously opposed by both New Haven and Milford, who claimed that the creation of a new town would deprive them of some of their lands, thereby weakening them, politically and economically. New Haven also contended that it would make too small a town. A charter was denied them.

In 1820 they approached the Ecclesiastical Society of North Milford with the proposition that the two districts unite in forming a town. The men of North Milford were very conservative.

First, they took a public opinion poll of the citizens. After much discussion, they agreed to join West Haven on three conditions:

1—"All town meetings and elector's meetings shall be at or near the meeting house in North Milford."

2—"That for the first ten years after the town shall have been organized, each Society shall pay such expenses as shall be incurred within its own limits in the way of town expenditures and concerns."

3—"That the Society of North Milford be at no pecuniary expense in case the General Assembly should not see cause to grant the petition for the new township."

Evidently these conditions were all accepted, and the General Assembly granted the charter. The charter and boundary lines given by the Assembly were as follows:

"At a general Assembly of the state of Connecticut holden at New Haven, in said state on the first Wednesday of May, in the year of our Lord one thousand eight hundred and twenty-two. Upon the petition of the Inhabitants of the Society of North Milford by their agents Ichabod Woodruff and others, and the inhabitants of the society of West Haven, by their agents, Nathan Platt and others, showing the population, situation, extent of territory and amount of Lists, etc. praying for reasons set forth at large in said petition; to be incorporated a distinct town; as by petition on file dated April 18, 1821.

"Resolved by this Assembly that all that part of the town of Milford known as North Milford, and that part of New Haven, within the following limits (to wit) beginning at the Sound, and extending through the harbour by the point of the Beach to the mouth of the West River, thence up said river in the center thereof to the bridge on the Derby Turnpike Road. Thence in a straight course westerly to Mixes North line, so called, thence in said Mixes line to Woodbridge line, thence in said Woodbridge line to Derby line, thence southerly on the Housatonic River, Thence in the line of the Society of North Milford to the line that divides the Society of West Haven from the town of Milford, and thence in the said last mentioned line to the Sound; with all the inhabitants residing within the said limits, be and the same is hereby incorporated into a distinct and separate Town by the name of Orange.

"And the inhabitants aforesaid and their successors forever residing within said limits shall have and enjoy all the powers, privileges and immunities enjoyed by other towns in this state, with the right of sending one Representative only to the General Assembly of this State. And said new town shall pay such proportion of all debts, charges and expenses, suits, petitions and claims already

34

due and accrued, commenced or existing against said Town of New Haven, or for which said town may hereafter be rendered liable by force of any claim now existing as (counting upon the List 1821) the amount of the List of the parish of West Haven and shall assume the care of the poor. The first town meeting shall be holden at the Meeting House in the Parish of North Milford, on the second Monday of June, next, at nine o'clock in the forenoon, and Charles H. Pond, Esq., and in case of his inability to attend, Charles Denison, Esq., shall be Moderator thereof, and shall warn such meeting by posting a warning on the public signpost in said town, and at such other publick place or places as he may think proper, at least six days before said first meeting.

"And all subsequent meetings shall holden at or near the Meeting House in the parish of North Milford.

"And said town of Orange shall have all the powers at said first meeting incident to the other towns in this state, and full right to act accordingly; and the officers elected at such meeting shall hold their offices until others are legally chosen and sworn in their stead."

May 28, 1822. A true copy, examined by Thomas Day.

The first town meeting was held on the second Monday, June, 1822. Charles H. Pond, Esq., high sheriff for the county of New Haven, Moderator.

The following gentlemen were chosen officers:

Town Clerk: Benjamin L. Lambert.

Selectmen: John Bryan, Jr., Thomas Painter, Ichabod A. Woodruff, Aaron Thomas, Jr., Lyman Law.

Treasurer: Nathan Clark.

Constables: Nathan Merwin, Lyman Prindle, Garry Treat, James Reynolds.

Grand Jurors: Nathan Clark, Jonathan Judd, John Hubbard, Nehemiah Kimberly.

Tythingmen: Garry Treat, Aaron Clark, Jr., Simeon Smith, Bradford Smith, Lyman Prindle, Samuel L. Pardee.

Sealers of Weights & Measures: Jesse Hodge, Filemon Smith.

Pound Keepers: Nathan Platt, Nathan Clark, James Reynolds.

Fence Viewers: Benjamin Clark, Jesse Allen, Jonas F. Merwin, Robert Treat, Jr., Eliakim Kimberly, Aaron Thomas, Jr.

The second town meeting was held October 7, 1822, at 2 o'clock. Thomas Painter, Esq., was chosen Moderator.

The Board of Assessors was then chosen.

They also voted that the official places to put up notices should be at North Milford, Allingtown and Dogburn.

On the second Monday of December, 1822, it was voted "that the Selectmen have the power of distributing the money at their discretion on the highways."

"Voted that a tax of six cents be laid on the dollar, including one and one-half cents for highways."

"Voted that the inhabitants have the liberty to work out their tax at eight cents an hour."

"Voted that Edmund K. Fowler be a Collector of State and Town tax with the encouragement of twenty dollars, by his giving sufficient security."

A committee had been appointed to select a name for the town. There was a difference of opinion; some wanted it North Milford, others favored Milford Haven, some liked Westford. Finally the committee chose Orange, in commemoration of the benefits received by the Colonists from William, Prince of Orange; particularly in the restoration of their charter privileges, after the tyranny of Sir Edmund Andros.

The first tax voted by the town in 1822 was high, six cents, or 60 mills, on the dollar; but the assessed valuation must have been very low, for the tax bills were very modest. Also, citizens could work out a part of their taxes on the highways, at eight cents an hour. This was under the Surveyors of Highways, who were paid at the same rate after they had worked out their own taxes. The office of tax collector was auctioned off to the lowest bidder. Nehemiah Woodruff owned a sizable farm in the Turkey Hill section; some of it was originally the Indian lands. His tax bill for 1837 was as follows:

To Town Tax on List of 1836, 5 per cent on $	$6.48
" State " " " " " " " " " "	1.30
	$7.78
Credit	3.24
	$4.54

The office of "fence-viewer" was taken rather seriously. All property owners were supposed to keep their fences in good condition. If a complaint was made, the fence-viewer notified the owner that he must put his fence in better order; if he failed to do this, the fence-viewers would have it repaired, sending the bill to the owner.

In 1822, Dr. Josiah M. Colburn, who had that year graduated from Yale, located here as a practicing physician. The record says that he continued here with much success until 1839, when he moved to Derby.

The very next year after the formation of the town, they resorted to the old New England custom of taking care of their poor. For, at the Town Meeting held October 6, 1823, it was voted, "that the Selectmen may put out the town paupers on the first Monday of November next, to be supported during the ensuing year; said disposal of them to be done at the house of Nathan Clark at one o'clock, p.m. They having received written and sealed proposals from individuals previous to said day." At a Town Meeting held October, 1825, it was voted that "the Selectmen examine the clothes of the town poor when taken by him or them who shall bid them off, and require them to be as well clothed when returned as when they take them."

At a special Town Meeting, November 20, 1823, the following action was taken: "Voted, that the Selectmen be required to notify all owners of land that has Canada Thistle growing thereon to remove the same as the statute directs; if neglected, to put the law in force."*

It was also voted that "geese found in any enclosure, not the owner's, are liable to be impounded at six cents per head."

"Voted that no swine be permitted to run in the highways over two months old, without a ring in the nose."

"Voted a bounty of six cents be paid for every crow or crow's head killed within the limits of the town, and delivered to the Selectmen."

Mention has previously been made of the hand-written book which was prepared by Rev. Erastus Scranton, entitled "Statistical Account, Town of Milford."

The following excerpts refer to Orange:

"There is no evidence that the planters of this town ever suffered for want of food or bread corn. . . . A majority of the wells in North Milford are dug ten to fifteen feet into a species of slate rock, mixt with white flint. And it is found to be about the same distance from the surface down to water in the valleys as on the hills and high ground . . . The principal productions of our ground are maize, rye, wheat, flax, oats, buckwheat, barley, potatoes, turnips, grass. Our lands are almost exclusively cultivated by oxen, or a joint team of oxen and a horse. Carts, only, instead of ox-wagons are made use of on the farms."

* An act to prevent the spreading of Canada Thistle was passed by the General Assembly: "All owners shall cut all fields or in highways containing Canada Thistle. No person shall plow any lands on which Thistle grows, if neglected, he shall pay a fine of $5.00 for every offense. If any grass seed sold could have Thistle in it, a fine of $10.00 will be imposed."

THE ORANGE GREEN

On January 9, 1812, Samuel Treat conveyed to Jonathan Rogers and Jonathan Treat, Committee of the North Milford Society, and the rest of the inhabitants of said society, land described as follows: One acre where the meeting house now stands, bounded east and south by highways; west and north by land of Samuel Treat; also one rod, more or less, bounded north and east by highways; south by land of said society, and west by land of Joseph Stone. The description of the second tract will be better understood when it is known that the Meeting House Lane, now running north of the parsonage, at that time ran south of the parsonage, and across what is now the center of the Green. It is believed that this road was changed about 1841.

On March 19, 1830, Erastus Scranton, the first pastor of the Orange Church, who owned considerable land near the Green, gave a deed as follows: "To Benjamin Clark, Nathan Clark, Josiah M. Colburn, and others of North Milford, in the town of Orange, and unto their posterity and future inhabitants, a tract of land bounded south and west by land of said Scranton; east by the highway and north by the Green, containing seventy-six rods; said land to be forever used or occupied as a part of a green, for the benefit or accommodation of the public in general; no building of any name or kind to be erected or to stand on said ground to the end of time. To have and to hold unto the said inhabitants of North Milford and other posterity or successors or residents of Orange."

On April 12, 1821, Benjamin Clark conveyed to Erastus Scranton and others, proprietors in the Academy of North Milford, the land on which it, the Academy, stands, about 24 feet long and 19 feet broad, with sufficient surrounding land for repairs, etc.; being north of my house and southeast of the meeting house in the place it was built in the year 1812, "to be used as an academical school for a common district school, for religious and public gatherings, and no other." This building stood on the ground now covered by the front of the present Town Hall, which was built in the winter and spring of 1879. The old Academy building was sold to Leverett B. Treat, who moved it down back of the house now owned by Elbert Scobie, where it was later destroyed by fire. John Bryan and his son, Richard, owned the property adjoining the southern end of the Green. On the east side of the Green, John Bryan kept a small store.[1] However, in 1838, Richard Bryan lost this property through bankruptcy, and it was sold at auction to Samuel Johnson. In 1841, Mr. Johnson sold the property to the North Milford Ecclesiastical Society, on which land the parsonage was built.

The Orange Church parsonage was bought under a co-operative plan. The property might be sold and the proceeds used for the support of the gospel; but if the property was used for any other purpose, it should revert to the American Board of Commissioners for Foreign Missions.

Samuel Treat owned much of the land on the hilltop north of the Green, where the church now stands, but he lived in what was in later years called Platt Valley, south of the house of the late Wellington M. Andrew. Calvin, son of Samuel Treat, settled in Ohio. It is related that twice he walked back and forth from Ohio, with an axe on his shoulder. On his first arrival there, he obtained a lively pair of oxen, hired a strong Negro, and together they smashed down the groves of black walnut they found there, and hauled the wood and timbers into heaps, for burning. This was to prepare the ground for wheat, which Mr. Treat made his chief crop for many years.

After the present church was built in Orange, the old meeting house was sold to Rev. Erastus Scranton for $101, and he had it moved across the street from its original location, to a place between the present Town Hall and the home of Benjamin T. Clark, and converted it into a dwelling. It was later destroyed by fire.

In 1851, Benjamin T. Clark sold a small strip of land, just west of the church, to nine persons, with the understanding that horse sheds should be built there. Later, in 1870, eleven more men bought enough land from Mr. Clark, so that two more rows of horsesheds were built, running north and south of the first row of sheds.

ORANGE BURIAL GROUND

In 1804, when the church was planned, they also set apart a half-acre of ground to be used as a burial ground; and the first one to be interred there was a baby, whose small headstone bears the following inscription:

> "In Memory of Joseph,
> child of Joseph and Eunice Treat,
> who died Nov. 2, 1805, aged 4 mo. 4 days.
>
> Behold the babe the Savior blest
> Enjoys the pleasure of his rest.
> I'm the 6th descent of this name
> And the first buried in this place."

The epitaphs on the earliest headstones are interesting. One wonders why they have such a melancholy tone. Of a young wife they say:

> Lucy, wife of Leverett Clark, died Aug. 23, 1847, aged 23 yrs.
>
> "She died as fair ones
> Often die, when bridal flowers
> Spring around their pathway
> but to deck their graves."

Evidently a tired housekeeper was accorded this tribute:

> Clarina, wife of Asa Alling, died Apr. 22, 1861, aged 78.
>
> "There shall I bathe my weary soul
> In seas of heavenly rest,
> And not a wave of trouble roll
> Across my peaceful breast."

Of a young girl, they have this sad refrain:

> Charlotte, daughter of Joseph and Charlotte Prudden
> died Aug. 13, 1843, aged 13 yrs.
>
> "Farewell dear friend, here you must lie
> But may not I when passing by
> Just drop a tear upon thy tomb
> Because thy sun has set so soon."

A story of tragedy is told on the headstone of Mr. Enoch Clark, Jr.:

> "In memory of Mr. Enoch Clark, Jr.
> who was instantly killed by lightning,
> whilst harvesting his grain, and found dead
> at midnight in his field.
> July 18, 1807, Aged 60.
> The Almighty God his dire thunder hurled
> Which called me instant to the other world.
> Ye mortals, heaven's eternal law obey
> Then Christ will own you at the judgement day."

But the most interesting family history is found on the headstones of Benjamin L. Lambert and his three wives. The first one is in memory of Anna, wife of Benjamin L. Lambert, who died January 22, 1815, aged 22.

> "A lovely daughter seven months old
> She left an afflicted father to console
> How sweet she shone in social life
> As daughter, sister, friend and wife.
> Her heart was formed for virtuous love
> We trust her soul now dwells with God above."

Right beside this stone is a similar stone with the following inscription:

> "In memory of Abigail, wife of Benj. L. Lambert,
> who died Dec. 8, 1816.
> "A lovely daughter four weeks old
> She left its afflicted father to console
> How sweet she shone in social life
> As daughter, sister, friend and wife.
> O reader, when these graces you see
> Think of death and eternity."

Next comes Mr. Lambert's stone, with this epitaph:

> "Benjamin L. Lambert, who died Oct. 11, 1825, aged 43.
> Six children of three different blood
> I leave them all in the hands of God,
> May they at last all meet above
> And sing the songs of redeeming love.
> Surviving partner, thou most dear
> Although I have two buried here
> Soon you must lie beside of me
> O then prepare for Eternity."

And last, the widow's stone bears this message:

> Eunice, widow of B. L. Lambert, who died June 27, 1845, aged 54.
> "Thou hast gone from us, dear mother,
> Thy voice no more we hear
> Thou hast left our kindred circle
> A brighter home to cheer."

Finally, the most brief and poignant epitaph is:

> George Merwin, son of Merwin and Elizabeth Andrew,
> died April 10, 1876, aged 9 yrs.
> "Papa, I'm coming"

EARLY MILITARY RECORDS OF ORANGE

For a small town, Orange may justly be proud of the record of its sons and daughters, too, when a call to the colors was urgent. The earliest military record we have was the commission of Joseph Treat to be Ensign of the first train band in Milford, in 1698. In 1704 he was a Lieutenant, and became Captain in 1708.

The next original document was issued to Captain Joseph Woodruff, of the 1st military company in Milford by Roger Newton, Colonel of the 2nd Regiment, on October 23, 1756, in which Captain Woodruff was ordered to recruit "five able bodied and effective men" to go forward to join the Army at Lake George. He was ordered to furnish each man "with a good blanket and firelock, and proper accoutrements; together with half a pound of powder, and a pound of bullets, unless any shall seasonable supply themselves."

The next commission was given by Thomas Fitch, Governor and Commander-in-Chief of His Majesty's Colony of Connecticut, May 1, 1762, and issued to Isaac Clark, informing him that he had been accepted by the General Assembly of this Colony to be a Lieutenant of the 2nd Company or Trainband, in the 2nd Regiment.

Another commission in the Colonial Army just prior to the Revolution was given by Jonathan Trumbull, Esq., Captain-General and Commander-in-Chief of his Majesty's Colony of Connecticut, to Isaac Treat, informing him that he had been chosen to serve as a Cornet* of the Troop of Horse in the 2nd Regiment in this Colony.

"Given under my hand and the Seal of this Colony, in Hartford, the 18th day of January in the 14th Year of the Reign of our Sovereign Lord George the Third, King of Great Britain, Etc. Annoque Domini 177/1."

Later Mr. Treat was promoted to Lieutenant, commanding a company of Light Horse, and did service around Milford during the Revolution.

The men from Orange who served in the Revolution and are buried in the Orange Cemetery were:

John Bryan	William Fowler	Stephen Russell
Aaron Clark	John Hine	Joseph Stone
Benjamin Clark	Miles Mallett	Samuel Stone
Isaac Clark	John Pardy	Joseph Treat
Robert Treat	Samuel Treat	

In 1739, it was ordered that the military companies of New Haven, Milford, Branford, and Derby be made into one entire regiment, the 2nd. Roger Newton was the Colonel of this regiment for many years.

Samuel Treat was appointed Ensign of the 2nd Company, 2nd Regiment, by the Assembly in October, 1768. He was promoted to Lieutenant in 1772, Captain in 1775, and advanced to Major of the 2nd Regiment in 1778. He resigned in 1779. He represented the Town as a member of the Legislature, 1783-84.

When the coast was threatened by the British fleet in 1776, Joseph Treat was especially valiant. On January 1, 1777, two hundred American soldiers were brought from British ships in New York harbor and suddenly landed from a cartel ship in Milford. Some of these soldiers were sick with small-pox; and Joseph Treat assisted in caring for them, having had the disease previously. Forty-six of these soldiers died.

In the War of 1812 were the following:

Enoch Clark	Samuel Potter	Benjamin Riggs
Nathan Merwin	Joseph Prudden	Jonathan Rogers

*A Cornet was the lowest commissioned officer in the English Cavalry Troops.

Isaac Porter was Captain of 3rd Company, Horse Artillery, for several years.

In the War Between the States, the Civil War, the men from Orange were mostly in the 15th Regiment or the 27th Regiment, Connecticut Volunteers. The 27th Regiment was in three of the hardest battles of the War. One-third of the Regiment was lost at the battle of Fredericksburg. Then came Chancellorsville, where several companies were taken prisoner; Company G, which included many Orange men, among them. They were taken to Libby Prison in Richmond, Virginia, but were later exchanged and returned to their homes at the expiration of their year's term of service. Then came Gettysburg, when half of those left in the 27th Regiment were lost.

A few men came into town after the close of the war and are buried in the cemetery. Their graves are always decorated on Memorial Day.

As far as is known, the complete list of names follows:

John H. Anthony	Eli A. Elvington	Henry S. Shaw
John H. Anthony, Jr.	H. Bliss French	Charles F. Smith
Allen D. Baldwin	Charles W. Hine	William G. Smith
Charles C. Baldwin	George W. Hungerford	Horace C. Stevens
Jared Baldwin	G. Fred Lowenstein	James Sullivan
Theodore Baldwin	Charles W. Pratorius	Charles H. Treat
Charles L. Beecher	Nathan Prudden	Dwight H. Treat
Joseph Casner	Azariah Riggs	Noyes A. Treat
Edwin Blakeman	Enoch E. Rogers	Thelus C. Treat
Albertus N. Clark	Elizur B. Russell	Theodore T. Warner
Dennis Clark	Stephen D. Russell	Stiles D. Woodruff
Everett B. Clark	William M. Russell	

There were two Gold Star members of the group. Dwight H. Treat, Company E, 7th Regiment, died at Port Royal, South Carolina, September 4, 1862, aged 17 years, and is buried in the Orange Cemetery.

Dennis Clark, Company E, 15th Regiment, died in battle and was brought home and buried from the Orange Church, April 12, 1863.

TURNPIKES IN ORANGE

The original meaning of the word *turnpike* was a barrier placed across a road to stop passage until the toll was paid; in other words, a toll-gate. Gradually the whole road on which a toll-gate was maintained was called a *turnpike*. There were two such roads in Orange.

THE DERBY TURNPIKE

The Derby Turnpike Company was formed in 1798. Its capital stock was about $7,500. There were ten original stockholders, and just one hundred shares were issued.

When Joseph Wheeler and others petitioned the General Assembly for a charter on the 2nd Thursday of May, 1798, it was stated that "the road now leading from Derby landing to the New Haven Court House is extremely bad, hilly, crooked and rough so as to be almost impassible for teams and carriages; that a new road or highway might be laid out from said landing to said Court house which would shorten the distance two miles, and be laid over good level and feasible land." Isaac Ticknor of Lebanon was the contractor who built the road, which was about eight miles in length, and was to be 18 feet wide, traveling part, at the rate of $2.00 per rod. There was a condition in the contract—"it is to be understood that where by reason of rocks or other obstructions it shall be extremely difficult to make the road 18 ft. wide, the party of the 2nd part shall make it as wide as the make of the ground shall admit."

The limits of the road were from "the house of Eneas Monson on York Street, New Haven, to the house of Joseph Wheeler, Derby landing." Derby was a prosperous village at this time, with quite an export trade, as ships came up the river from foreign ports, especially the West Indies.

In his history of Derby, Orcutt tells of the disappointment of the man who worked so hard to get the road and helped build it at great expense. He had an extensive trade, which he expected would be increased; but instead, after

46

the road was made a Turnpike, he was obliged to watch all the trade pass him by and go to New Haven. The toll-gate was located in Orange, near the Maltby Lakes. For the first fifty years, the gate-keeper was Mrs. Mary Pardee,

TOLL-GATE AND HOUSE, DERBY TURNPIKE[2]
Courtesy of Walter E. Malley

who was succeeded by Mrs. Mary Beardsley. The gate-keeper best known to the older residents of the town was Miss Fannie Beardsley, who lived in the house beside the toll-gate with her grandmother. Certain exemptions were allowed. "Persons traveling to and from public worship, funerals, or society, town or freeman's meetings, persons obliged to do military duty, traveling to and from train-ing, persons going to and from grist mills with grists, and farmers who shall pass through the same to attend to their ordinary farming business shall not be liable to the payment of said toll." But the gate-keeper was some-what skeptical when the young men claimed they were going to meeting, for she didn't believe that they held a prayer meeting every night in New Haven.

There was much opposition to selling the land for the right of way when the project was first started, and one Edward Alling challenged the would-be buyers at the point of his pitch-fork. Eventually he did sell, but only

47

RATES of TOLL.

		Cts.	M.
Every Travelling 4 Wheel PLEASURE CARRIAGE		25	
do Mail Stage		25	
" Other " "		25	
" Carriage drawn by 1 Horse and the body hung on springs of Iron. Steel. or Leather		12.5	
" 1 Horse Pleasure Wagon		.08	
" Chaise. Chair or Sulkey		.12.5	
" Loaded Wagon or Cart		.12.5	
" Empty " " "		.06.2½	
" Single Horse Cart or W. loaded		.06.2½	
" " " " " " empty		.06.2½	
" Pleasure Sleigh		.06.2½	
" Loaded " or Sled		.06.2½	
" Empty " " "		.03	
" Person and Horse		.04	
" Horse Cattle or Mule		.01	
" Sheep and Hogs		.00.5	

because he obtained the concession of a lower toll for himself and his neighbors. One historian, in speaking of the boundaries of this road, gave the measurements by chains and links.

At a Town Meeting on October 1, 1887, a resolution was passed that the "Selectmen be authorized to hire the New Haven and Derby Turnpike for the free use of the inhabitants of Orange for a sum not to exceed $240 each year, for a period of five years."

The sign-board which hung on the side of the house, showing the different rates of toll, is now in the New Haven Colony Historical Society on Whitney Avenue, New Haven.

It was always just an ordinary dirt road, and almost impassible in the Spring of the year when the frost was coming out of the ground. When the road was discontinued as a toll-road in 1897, the different towns paid the company certain sums of money for the right of way. Orange paid $800.

The road usually paid its stockholders at the rate of six per-cent. interest. A final dividend of $67.78 per share was declared on its one hundred shares on June 21, 1897, just one year short of a hundred years of existence.

Having acquired the Turnpike at a Town Meeting held April 15, 1897, they voted "that $3000 be appropriated in making improvements on the highway known as the Derby Turnpike."

TAVERNS

In the days of stage coaches, it was necessary to have taverns, conveneintly located, where the passengers, and the horses, too, could rest on the journey. There were three such taverns on the Derby Turnpike, only one of which is in use now.

One of them stood at the corner of College Road, which was owned by the Alling family, later the home of Theron Alling for many years. It was destroyed by fire some years ago. On the old maps, this was marked as "halfway house." Another was called Sun-rise Tavern and was

49

ALLING HOUSE, FORMERLY A TAVERN

—Photo by Jonathan Rogers

run by Andrew P. Hine[3] He had a very fancy sign-board which marked the place. Part of that house still stands, a grim reminder of former usefulness. It underwent a major operation when the Wilbur Cross Parkway was constructed and lost the front half of the building[4]

The house by the Wepawaug dam, occupied by the care-taker of the New Haven Water Company, was once a tavern. There are two enormous chimneys. The one on the east side of the house had a large Dutch oven. On the west side is a closet between the front and back rooms, with a window in it. This was used to serve the tap room. This house was in the Alling family for generations.

THE MILFORD TURNPIKE

In 1802, the New Haven and Milford Turnpike Company was organized. Of particular interest was the fact that it was ordered to have one gate, wherever three Judges of the County Court should direct. One hundred shares of capital stock were issued.

In his history, Lambert says: "At a town meeting, it was voted to oppose the New Haven and Milford Turnpike Company running the turnpike through people's land, also voted that it must follow the roadways, except to cut sharp corners."

The toll-gate on this road was also in Orange, located near the underpass of the old railroad between New Haven and Derby. For many years Mr. Benjamin Somers was the gate-keeper, living in a small house near by. Later he moved to Orange Center, to the house just south of the Cemetery, now owned by Arthur W. Chambers, Jr. As this Turnpike was a link in the post line between Boston and New York, it occupied a place of importance. After the railroad between New Haven and New York was built, with the first trains starting in December, 1848, traffic on the Turnpike began to decline. At a Town meeting held October 6, 1873, Orange voted "to purchase the stock of the Milford Turnpike Company, exclusive of the toll-gate property, for a sum not to exceed $500."

The tavern on this Turnpike has had a very checkered career.

Woodruff's Tavern, or Half-Way House

The history of this property goes back to the early days of the town. There is no tradition that George Washington ever stopped there, but it is full of history.

The last name on the list of "free planters" of Milford is William East. Mr. East's first wife died, and in 1675 he married a widow, Mrs. Mary Plum. It was some of his estate which he gave to her that became the Tavern, or, as it is better known, Half-way House. Mary East left some property to her grandson, John Woodruff. In 1767 John conveyed his property to his son, Enoch, "with my new house where Enoch now lives, at a place called Half-way Tree." So it would appear that the original house was built around 1767. When Enoch Woodruff's estate was distributed in 1787, he left dower rights in the house to his widow and to each of his four children. To his daughter, Polly, he left the "bar room," and to both Polly and Anne were given "a large quantity of rum," which suggests that the house may have been a public house before the Milford Turnpike was built in 1801. Polly (whose real name was Mary) married William Woodruff. It clearly appears that at that time the house had been built in three sections, the middle part being brick, and high up on the brick part the name of William Woodruff was painted in large letters. In the heyday of its existence, the Tavern was the scene of much gaiety, as frequent references are found concerning the balls and other social events held at Woodruff's Tavern.

After 1850 its popularity began to decline, for the railroad between Boston and New York was well established, so we assume the tavern business and coaching trade had greatly diminished. After 1858 this property, consisting of several pieces, including the tavern, changed hands twelve times, finally being acquired in 1897 by Arthur S. Crosby. He remodelled the house extensively and lived there for over forty years after which it was sold to Mary and Albert Sylvia, the present owners. The additions which were put on did not conform to the original style of architecture and did not improve its appearance, but it still caters to the traveler, as it is now maintained as a "Tourist Home."

Before we leave the subject of the Half-way House, we might note in passing that in his history of Milford, Mr. Scranton says: "Mary Ann Luce, a French woman, stabbed a knife into her breast, left side, at Mrs. Woodruff's Inn, in consequence of which she died in thirty minutes, A.D. 1814."

OLD HOUSES

The oldest house in the town, as previously mentioned, is supposed to have been built around 1720 by Richard Bryan, a grandson of Alexander Bryan, one of the original "Planters." It is now the home of Miss Virginia N. Rhodes. The house has retained its original lines, with its long, sloping roof. The outstanding feature is the massive fireplace which takes up nearly one whole side of the room which was probably the kitchen.

ISAAC TREAT HOUSE

The Isaac Treat house on Grassy Hill is a fine example of early architecture, and has been kept or restored to its original lines. The house was started before the Revolutionary War, but had to wait for over two years for its completion because the blacksmith who was making the nails went off to the War, so nothing could be done until his return. At a south-east window of the attic was a loft or lookout to watch for Indians. On a joist in the attic there were recently found a slipper and a little bundle of switches, an old custom observed in building, as a guarantee of happiness for the young couple who were to occupy the house.

The present owner is John F. Single, Jr.

RICHARD BRYAN HOUSE
—*Photo by Jonathan Rogers*

ISAAC TREAT HOUSE
—*Photo by Jonathan Rogers*

EDMUND FOWLER HOUSE
—Photo by Jonathan Rogers

P. MAXWELL HOUSE
—Photo by Jonathan Rogers

NEHEMIAH WOODRUFF HOUSE
TURKEY HILL

COLONEL ASA PLATT HOUSE
—*Photo by Jonathan Rogers*

LEWIS BRADLEY HOUSE

The Bradley house on Race Brook Road must have been built prior to 1800. The exterior of the house has been changed so that it has lost its original style of architecture. However, a picture is in existence, showing the way it used to look. It has a massive fireplace in the kitchen, which shows that the house was built long years ago. The Bradley farm was part of the plot which became Tyler City. It now beyongs to William A. Knight.

COLONEL ASA PLATT HOUSE

Still another fine type of early architecture was the house built in 1810 by Colonel Asa Platt. It stands at the corner of Race Brook Road and Tyler City Road. This was built to be a show place, to be used as an inn. The carving and paneling are especially good, and there are numerous spacious rooms. Originally there was a lookout on the roof.

But the Colonel met with financial difficulties and was forced to dispose of the property through foreclosure. In 1840 it was bought by William Ell Russell, and has been in the Russell family ever since that time. At present it is occupied by Clarence and Inez Russell Hall. There are some amusing anecdotes connected with this house.

At one time there was to be a wedding. The bride was all dressed in her wedding finery, the guests were all assembled. But when the appointed hour arrived, the bride was missing. They searched high and low. Finally she was discovered hiding behind a huge iron pot out in the shed. When pressed for an explanation, she said that she had found out that the wedding cake wasn't quite done, so she had taken this method of delaying the ceremony until everything was ready.

Because of its size, in later years some of the town poor were boarded in this house. One day, during a terrific downpour of rain, one of these paupers was discovered out-of-doors, under the eaves, getting the full benefit of the storm. She explained that she was trying to wash Satan out of her soul.

Around 1800, or a few years prior to that date, there must have been quite a building boom in the town, as there are numerous houses, still in fine condition, which must have been erected in that period. Most of them bear the conventional Colonial lines, but two or three have a different style of architecture. Several of these houses face the Green. The Edward L. Clark house was built in 1771.

The children of Frederick J. Hine are the ninth generation of Hines to live in the house on the Derby Turnpike, which was originally built by Samuel Hine.

Jonathan Rogers's house, south of the Green, was built in 1803. However, through the years additions or alterations have robbed some of these homes of their original, simple lines.

The age of the Nehemiah Woodruff house is not exactly known, but it was certainly built prior to 1800. On the deeds of this property, some of the boundary lines read: "bounded on the west by the Indian lands." The land reserved for the Indians in Turkey Hill was adjacent to this property.

MINERAL DEPOSITS

Some of the early historians seemed to think that there were signs of mineral deposits in different sections of the town. In fact, the early map lists a place designated as "asbestous rocks." We quote from Lambert's "History of the Colony of New Haven" — "In this parish, about twenty years ago (1818) a deposit of galena and silver was found on land now owned by Mr. John Lambert, lying on the old country road. It was discovered by David Lambert, the father of the present owner, by digging in a fox burrow. He obtained a considerable quantity of ore, but having a large farm which required his attention, he did not long continue to work it.

"Copper has lately been found in the same range of

rocks by the New York Mining Company. The ore raised is chiefly yellow copper pyrites, associated with variegated copper, and faint arborization of native copper. Copper pyrites are found in similar circumstances near the three-mile gate, on the Milford Turnpike. Asbestos is abundant in the serpentine rocks which abound in the southern section of the Township."

In the early days of the town, there were at least a dozen or more Negro slaves, who were treated more as members of the family. Some of them were given their freedom upon the death of their master; otherwise they were handed down to the children of the family. If they had not been freed before, they all obtained their freedom in 1848, when the state legislature passed a bill abolishing slavery in the State of Connecticut. The deeds of sale, which read like the sale of real estate, are interesting souvenirs kept by some of the citizens. The sale price varies from "fifty pounds, lawful money" to one who was sold for "twenty barrels of merchantable pork."

Joseph Treat owned two slaves, whom he inherited from his father. One of these was always called "Clock Tom" because every day at noon he blew a conch shell from the roof of the house, giving the time to that part of town. This was regulated by his master's brass clock, which was at that time the only one in North Milford. So, in a way, he was the forerunner of the radio announcer.

Samuel Prudden, a direct descendent of Rev. Peter Prudden, also owned a slave. He lived at the place now owned by Everett B. Clark, II. The story is told that once Mrs. Prudden was ill, so she sent her servant to a neighbor's to borrow some metheglin, or mead, which was a drink made of honey and water, fermented by yeast, a very popular Colonial beverage. When the girl returned, there was a very small quantity in the bottle, so her mistress accused her of drinking it. Whether the girl was guilty is not told; however, she was so indignant at being blamed that she went out and set fire to the house, which was totally destroyed. Mr. Prudden rebuilt on the same foundation, which building was later moved back and converted into a barn to make room for the present house. Samuel Prudden was a valuable member of the Orange Church.

THE EARLY SCHOOLS

The need of adequate facilities for teaching the children was demonstrated in the early days of the town, for it is recorded that at a Town Meeting held in Milford, December 10, 1750, it was "voted that money should be appropriated to the inhabitants of Bryan's Farms, for the purpose of setting up a school in winter, it being so well settled that one is deemed necessary." Where this early school was located is unknown.

As soon as the Church was organized, they set about establishing a school system. The first meeting of the North Milford School Society was held on November 6, 1806. The section was divided into three districts: the southern part was called the First District, the northern part was called the Second District, and the western part was called the Third District. Jonah Treat was chosen to serve as committee-man from the First District, David Treat, 2nd, for the Second, and Benjamin Fenn for the Third District. These districts were set off from Milford, and after much discussion, the sum of $599 from the Milford budget was allowed for the expenses of the year. A committee-man was chosen for each district, who was to make the arrangements for said district, supply the teacher, and see that the necessary supply of wood was available. A committee, composed of the leading men of the town, was chosen to act as school visitors, who were to visit the schools and pass judgment on them. Very simple school houses were built, with wood used to supply the heat.

No special preparation seemed necessary to qualify as a teacher. After the formation of the Town of Orange, the Allingtown section was added to the School Society and was called the Fourth District. In 1882 some of the

THE ORANGE HIGH SCHOOL IN 1891
Miss Bachelder, Teacher. [5]

SECOND DISTRICT SCHOOL, ABOUT 1890.
Miss Fannie Pardee, Teacher.

families who lived nearer the Milford boundary asked to be included in the Milford district, as that school was much nearer to their homes. This petition was granted, and the Orange districts were reorganized. The First District remained as originally planned, to include the southern part of the town; the Second District was to cover the northwestern section; and the Third District was the northeastern part of the town. The First District schoolhouse was at the corner of Orange Center Road and Old Tavern Road. The first schoolhouse of the Second District was at a triangle formed by the junction of Grassy Hill Road and the Milford Road.[6] The Third District schoolhouse was originally on the west side of Race Brook Road, on land now included in the Country Club grounds. The districts had made it a rule that no pupil over sixteen years of age should be admitted to the schools.

About 1812 the old Academy was built on the grounds now occupied by the Town Hall. This was a two-story building with a cupola, and was at first called the "Winter School." While there is no visible proof for this statement, still it would appear that this school required a small tuition on the part of the pupil, and was for older students. There is no reference of expenditures of money by the Town excepting for the district schools. At several of the meetings of the School Society, there were attempts made to get an appropriation for "a school of higher order," but these were always voted down.

The Academy school was held on the second floor, while the first floor was used as an assembly room. The School Society meetings were always held here, as well as the singing school. It was also used for smaller meetings of the Church, and for the "preparatory lecture" which was always held on the Friday afternoon preceding the Communion Service of the Church.

Isaac Platt Treat and Benjamin T. Clark were teachers or schoolmasters at various times. It was said their hardest task was to sharpen the goose quills, which had to be done every day, as writing and reading were considered the

62

most important branches of learning. In the records of the Third District are found the specifications for their school house. On June 9, 1829, they voted to build a house twenty-four feet long and sixteen feet wide, covered with pine boards on the sides and ends with good shingles on the roof. It was to have an oak floor, the inside sealed with pine boards, and the house was to be well lighted. Also they favored an open stove in preference to a chimney.

The custom followed in the districts was to have a winter school beginning the middle of November, to run for four months, and to employ a man teacher; and a summer school beginning the middle of April and continuing for six months, with a woman as teacher. Also, the teacher was supposed to board around with the inhabitants of the district. Anyone who refused to board his proportion was taxed at the rate of $1.25 per week. In 1837 the Third District voted "to engage Charles Wheeler to teach the winter school at $30 or less per month." From all accounts, Mr. Wheeler's outstanding proficiency was his use of the rod. The matter of discipline came up for consideration, too. The district voted: "In case a scholar becomes disobedient, the teacher shall use the rod, if he thinks proper, once or twice. If that does not succeed, the scholar shall be expelled, and not permitted to rejoin until they shall have made suitable acknowledgement in the presence of the school and the teacher, and that this be read to the school." The scope of the business which was considered by the School Society was very varied. For instance, in the call for the Annual Meeting of the School Society to be held October 3, 1836, it was "to transact the regular business of the society, also to take into consideration the expediency of repairing the fence to the burying ground, and to purchase a hearse for the School Society." This action was passed in the affirmative, after which it was voted "to tax ourselves 1½ cents on the dollar on the list of 1835 to pay for it."

Some controversy arose about the boundary lines or the district tax in the Second District. The distance to the school was rather long for some pupils, so at a School

Society Meeting December 1, 1834, a new district was formed, called the Fourth District, and soon after a schoolhouse was built in that section of the town, near the Wepauwaug River, where nearly every family bore the name of Clark, which section has ever since been known as "Clarktown." After this division, it was eventually decided to move the location of the Second District schoolhouse. The old schoolhouse was sold to Merritt Pardee for $30 and moved up to his premises, and a new plot of ground, corner of Ridge Road and Old Grassy Hill Road, was bought from Lyman Treat for $50. The new schoolhouse was built, with Miss Martha Miles the first teacher.

There was evidently a call to use the schoolhouses on Sunday, for on November 3, 1836, they voted that religious meetings could be held in the schoolhouses on Sabbath days, provided that two cupboards were furnished to hold the school books, without any expense to the district.

In 1848 the Second District paid Miss Caroline Russell $27.50 for teaching school for 22 weeks. Dennis Andrew was paid $3.00 for boarding the teacher for two weeks. The system of the length of the terms was changed in 1851. Instead of a summer and a winter term, the year was divided into three terms, the winter term to consist of twelve weeks and the spring and fall terms to be fourteen weeks each, and the committee was instructed to obtain teachers from the Normal School if possible.

This same year, legal complications seemed to have developed regarding the land on which the Third District house was built. Rather than take it to court, the best way out of the controversy appeared to be to sell the old schoolhouse to A. H. and C. B. Alling for $38 and secure a new location on the other side of the street, on which they built a new schoolhouse, taxing the property of the district in order to pay the bill.

On October 23, 1855, the School Society decided that they needed a new hearse. Accordingly, they voted to sell the old hearse and harness and buy a new hearse and harness, taxing themselves 1¼ cents on the dollar on the list of 1855 to pay for it. A small building had been built in the rear of the cemetery, where the hearse was kept. It was also ordered that Alpheus N. Merwin take charge of the hearse and go with it when called upon to attend funerals, collecting his pay from the persons who required his services.

At the same time they voted to pay $120 to Benjamin T. Clark for an acre of land to enlarge the cemetery. This vote was later rescinded, as the land was bought by the Town and not by the School Society.

By 1859 it was found that the First District needed a new schoolhouse, so they voted to build one as near as possible to the location of the old building. In all these carefully-kept records, extending for over a hundred years, never once was there any mention made of the number of pupils in the schools, and very few of the teachers are named.

Much has been written in song and legend about "the little red schoolhouse," but as far as can be learned, the schoolhouses in Orange were always painted white.

Notes

1. Richard Bryan's store was located on the west side of the Green, not the east side as Miss Woodruff noted.

2. According to *History of Orange: Sesquicentennial 1822 - 1972*, the toll house on the Derby Turnpike near Maltby Lake also served as Everett's Tavern.

3. The Sunrise Tavern operated by Andrew Hine was located just west of the current intersection of the Derby Turnpike (Route 34) and Racebrook Road. The exterior of the tavern still remains, but it has been completely remodeled inside by its current owners, The Legions of Christ, as an education center. The adjacent gristmill and sawmill were destroyed by an ice release in the 1800s.

4. Woodruff is confusing the Sunrise Tavern with the home of "Patsy" McDermott, a jockey who maintained a small track on his property further down on Route 34 for training and racing. The State of Connecticut approached the property's subsequent owners about purchasing the house in order to widen Route 34. When the State failed to pay the desired price, the owners took down half of the house north of the line and left the rest standing with blank walls facing the new Derby Turnpike. It remained in that condition for many years until the property was finally developed as Green Circle.

5. Mary Rebecca Woodruff, the author of the *History of Orange, North Milford, 1639 - 1949,* is seen here as a 15-year-old seated in the front row at the Orange High School (the Academy), second from left. As the young ladies are holding hats and wearing flowers, it may signify their graduation. There is strong evidence that Mary went on to a boarding school in Massachusetts in the 1890s before enrolling at Oberlin College in Oberlin, Ohio in 1897. She left the college's arts and sciences program after her freshman year for unknown reasons.

6. The Grassy Hill Road Woodruff refers to here is now known as Old Grassy Hill Road.

The Middle Years [1]

PART III.

EARLY INDUSTRIES

MILLS RUN BY WATER POWER

AS in other towns in New England during a part of the eighteenth century and through the nineteenth century, water power was utilized in Orange, particularly on the Wepawaug, although to some extent Race Brook and branches of the Indian River contributed. As far back as 1776, Garett N. Dewitt had a saw mill at the place where the Derby Turnpike crosses the stream. Whether he built it or bought it from others does not appear in the record. At about the same place, Zeri Alling had a grist mill, which was called "the old red mill." He ground into flour the rye and buckwheat grown by the farmers. For payment he retained a certain portion of the flour—a most generous portion, so the farmers thought. He also ground yellow corn into meal. When cooked, this dish was called "samp." This miller also kept a pen of hogs, and because of the abundance of feed, his animals were larger and fatter than any others.

On March 5, 1819, Amos Alling became the owner of the mill run by Garrett Dewitt. His son, Charles W. Alling, succeeded him on March 26, 1834. Before many years, the son enlarged the scope of the business by building a mill for weaving cloth. At that time the spinning-wheel and hand-loom were chiefly depended upon to clothe the people. One person who used to go around to the houses with her hand-loom was called "Aunt Parney." She was very indignant at Mr. Alling for starting a factory, for she claimed he was taking away her livelihood. In 1823 Mr. Alling built a three-story building for dressing cloth and carding wool. This gave employment to thirty-five or forty people. In 1840, six years after his

67

son, Charles Willis Alling, succeeded him, a new mill was built, introducing spinning-looms, enabling them to weave cloth.

For many years the section around the Alling mills was called Jerusalem. As far as can be learned, this name came from a chance remark one day by the elder Mr. Alling. The mill people had many children, and, noticing them out playing one day, he said, "Why it is like the children playing in the streets of Jerusalem." So from that day on, it was "Jerusalem." Later Mr. Alling took his two sons, Amos H. and Charles B. Alling, into the business with him. They carried on the business there until 1759, when they moved to Birmingham, later called Derby, and built a much larger mill.[2]

The mill in Orange was left to be run by a younger brother, Leonidas W. Alling. During the Civil War, cloth for Union soldier uniforms was made in this factory. This mill was destroyed by fire in 1900. The story is told about a practical joker, named Crofut, who one day said to the girls who worked in the Alling mills, "Want to see some fireworks? Well, just look out the window." Lying outside the saw mill across the street there was a log, which had evidently been rejected, for it had lain there for some time. Mr. Crofut thought he could blow it up; so he bored a hole in it, inserted some powder, lighted it, and then backed away to await developments. Nothing happened, so he went over, got astride the log, and leaned over to blow up a flame. Suddenly the charge went off, and he went up with it. His little experiment cost him the loss of an eye.

On July 27, 1827, Stephen Twining conveyed to Henry Fitts and Lewis Gilbert mill property situated on the Wepawaug, a little south of the Alling mills. The deed describes a dwelling, barn, saw mill, fulling mill, carding shop, dye shop, and grist mill. There was no road near the property, as Mapledale Avenue had not been put through at that time. After 1850 this property fell into disuse, and in 1863 it was conveyed to a son of Charles W. Alling.

February 4, 1835, Aaron Clark and his wife, Elizabeth, deeded their son Aaron, Jr., twenty-two acres, reaching westerly to the Wepawaug River. This property was located about half a mile below the Alling property. There was no mention of mills, but in 1858 rights in mills were deeded to Timothy Perkins, and it is known that at this place there was a saw mill, a mill to make stocking yarn, and a wheelwright's shop, which were probably built about the time or a little later than the conveyance to Aaron, Jr. The only means of reaching these mills, also, was cross-lots from the Orange Center Road. Aaron, Jr., was a very skillful man, and it is believed that he was able to construct the large over-shot and under-shot water wheels used at that time.

A mile or so south on the same Wepawaug River, there was a saw mill maintained by Deacon Joseph Treat. His house and barn were close by on the little road known as Wepawaug Lane, very near the original Second District schoolhouse.

Parson Hine had a grist mill on Race Brook, where the attractive Overbrook property is now located. He ground corn for cattle; he also had a circular saw for sawing wood. This mill was destroyed in a freshet in 1869. Like most water mills in New England, all these mills have disappeared. What remained of the Twining mills was burned in 1870.

At a special Town Meeting held April 3, 1837, a petition was presented by Aaron Clark, Jr., and others to lay a new road, commencing at the bend of the road near the dwelling house of Jonathan Treat (present home of Arthur D. Clark), running in a northerly direction to the saw mill of Aaron Clark, Jr., thence to the carding and cloth-dressing establishment of Messrs. Fitt and Twining, extending on and intersecting the Derby Turnpike road near the home of Charles W. Alling. This petition was accepted, but as always happens when a new road is proposed, the difficulty came when title to the land was sought. It took months of litigation in the courts before clear title was obtained and the road known as Mapledale Avenue was built.

THE CHURCH CHANGES ITS NAME

The church services at this time were long. There was a very long prayer, followed by an extremely long sermon; but there is no record of any heat in the church, excepting the scant comfort supplied by a foot warmer, until the latter part of 1831, when they voted to procure a stove, and the committee were ordered to furnish wood at the expense of the Ecclesiastical Society. In 1838 they voted that individuals should have the privilege of building horse sheds. By a petition to the General Assembly in 1841, the name of the Society was officially changed from the Ecclesiastical Society of North Milford to that of Orange. The same year a parsonage was built for the use of the pastor.

One of the outstanding events of the year 1843 was the great revival. At that time the Church had no settled pastor. A Baptist minister, Rev. Mr. Waterbury, wanted to hold revival meetings in the church. This was not considered best, but the Fourth District schoolhouse was offered, and a large tent was added to accommodate the crowds that came. That January was like Indian Summer: no fires were needed, and the bare ground had no chill as people knelt upon it. A great comet blazed from the zenith to the horizon and terrified the hearts of the congregation. It was said that the whole town was converted. At any rate, when Rev. Cyrus Brewster was called to the pastorate of the Church in the Spring, he had the unusual joy of welcoming eighty new members at his first Communion Service.

In December of that year, the duties of sexton were plainly stated: "the duties of sexton for this society shall be to ring the bell for all meetings of this church and society and toll it for the death of any of its members. To sweep the house, properly, make the fire and light the house for all religious meetings. Take down the stove and pipe in the Spring. Clean, black and put the stove and pipe back in its place in the Fall. Also to make the fire and light the Academy for all religious and singing meetings; take down the stove and pipe and replace them when required, and sweep the Academy when necessary, and to be under the inspection of the Society's committee." The position of sexton was auctioned off, and this year it was bid off by William T. Grant for $19.50 for the year's work.

The Ecclesiastical Society hired the use of the lower room in the Academy for $5.00 a year. They met here for smaller meetings and for the singing school, which they continued for years, appropriating $50.00 annually to pay a singing instructor. That the people of that day were conservative is borne out in an article that appeared in the *New Haven Journal-Courier* February 10, 1848.

FAIR IN ORANGE

"The ladies of the Congregational Church in Orange hold a fair at the house of D. B. Stone, Esq., this and tomorrow afternoon and evening, commencing at two o'clock. The object is a worthy one and we trust our citizens will call on the ladies with their contributions. It is a most awful whiggish place, but the women are pretty, and compound capital cake."

Those early Sabbaths were kept holy. At sunset on Saturday night all work and play ended, and the Sabbath was one long day of peace and rest. The hours must have seemed terribly long to the children, but most parents insisted on strict obedience. One of the town's most distinguished women, Miss Emily Prudden, told the story of one Sunday when all homes were closed by a raging snow storm. The snow was above the fences, and some one was sent to bring the sheep to a place of safety. As the sheep came tumbling over the fence, they looked like snow banks, jumping up and down. Glad of something to break the quiet, the children shouted for joy as they watched the sheep. But they were reprimanded by their father: "Hush, hush, I should think it was Training Day." And he made the children sit in chairs in the back of the room, to help them keep quiet on Sunday.

One of the Church's most revered Deacons was Calvin Beach, who served in that capacity for many years. He was such a regular attendant at church that even his old horse caught the spirit. It was told that one Sunday when the good Deacon was too ill to go to church, the old horse heard the church bell ring, and, since no one had come to get him, he jumped the fence, trotted to church, and took his accustomed place in the horse sheds.

FIRST TOWN HALL

All of the town meetings and elector's meetings were held in the meeting house of the North Milford Church for the first twenty-five years. In 1835 permission was granted by the General Assembly to strike out the clause in the original charter, which decreed "that all meetings of the town shall be held at or near the meeting house of North Milford." However, they continued to be held there until May 22, 1848, when a special Town Meeting was called to be held at William Woodruff's Tavern. At this meeting it was voted that a small Town Hall should be built, as near William Woodruff's as possible. A building committee was appointed who were instructed to have the building completed by October 1. This Town Hall was used for the next forty years.

By an act of the Legislature on June 25, 1869, the Town was divided into two voting districts—"That portion of the town within the limits of the North, Union and West school districts shall be and remain the First District. That portion within the limits of the 1st, 2nd, 3rd, and 4th school districts shall be the Second voting District." After the erection of the new Town Hall in West Haven in 1893, the town meetings were held in that building.

TOWN RECORDS

As far as can be learned, the early town records were kept in a pine box in a house on the Milford Turnpike which was known as the Ruth Farm. That house was destroyed by fire some years ago. When Elias T. Main was elected Town Clerk in 1858, the records were moved to his house, which was also on the Milford Turnpike. Later a small second-hand safe was procured to provide better protection for valuable papers. A Town Clerk's office was established in West Haven in 1874 in a central building, and the safe was moved to that office.

When the West Haven Town Hall was erected in 1892, a fire-proof vault was provided to hold all records pertaining to the Town. All early records are deposited there, and up to the year 1921, when the towns were separated.

The Town Clerk's office and all records were kept in the home of Arthur D. Clark for the next twenty-five years, until Mr. Clark retired from the office of Town Clerk.

At the present time, the Town Clerk's office is at the Town Hall, with a specially-built room designated as the "safe room" to hold all records. The present Town Clerk is Howard B. Treat.

IRA CLARK MURDER

Whether or not crime was more prevalent in the earlier days, it seems to be certain that the facilities for detecting it were much less effectual than at the present time. This is illustrated by the Ira Clark murder. Ira Clark, with his wife and children, lived on the road from Milford to Derby, just below what was known as "George's Cellar Hill." They had a boarder by the name of Bowen. Bowen and the wife became very friendly, so much so that the husband became an incumbrance, and on the morning of the 18th of September, 1850, he was found behind the barn, with his throat cut. Traces of blood were found in the kitchen. On that morning, Bowen hitched up his horse and drove to the house of Gould Smith, who was a grand juror, to inform him of the murder. Bowen was arrested by Dennis Stone, a constable who lived in the house directly across from the church (now occupied by Mr. and Mrs. Harry Olsson). The arrest was made so late in the week that he was obliged to hold his prisoner over Sunday, and having no lockup, he kept him with him in his house. Mr. Stone was not accustomed to attending church, but on that Sunday he went to church, taking his prisoner with him. He selected one of the front pews, where everyone could see him. The pulpit was occupied that day by a Rev. Mr. Carpenter from Birmingham (now Derby). Public sentiment was greatly stirred, and suspicion was running high against the prisoner. Knowing this, and assuming that the prisoner was guilty, the preacher took the opportunity to address him from the pulpit in scathing terms.

The following day E. K. Foster, who has been called one of the ablest State's Attorneys in the County, was called in to prosecute the case, to determine whether the accused should be bound over for trial. This he did in the Orange Church, with an insistent crowd of citizens about him. But the prisoner was discharged. The State's Attorney said he thought the Orange people were the most unreasonable set of beings he had ever met. They had an intuitive conviction that the prisoner was guilty, but to him they seemed an unreasoning mob. As he left the church after his acquittal, Bowen noticed in the crowd on the steps the minister who had preached at him the day before, so he approached him saying: "I don't know any reason why I shouldn't punch you in the nose."

Eventually Bowen and the wife left town, and Alanson, brother of Ira Clark, took the four children to his home to live.

On the morning when Bowen drove to the house of the grand juror, it was found, by following the tracks of his wagon, that he stopped and tied his horse to a fence at George's Cellar Hill. Search was made along the wall on the side on which he had tied his horse, but nothing was found. Before the murder Bowen was accustomed to wearing a suit of clothes of noticeable color and appearance. After the murder he was never seen to wear it.

Years after the tragedy, when Bowen had disappeared and perhaps died, in overhauling an old wall on the opposite side of the road from where Bowen tied his horse that fatal morning, William Prudden and his man pulled from the wall the long sought-for suit of clothes, all spattered with stains which they assumed could only be blood. Many years later, after being abandoned by Bowen, and sick and destitute, Mrs. Ira Clark came back to her brother-in-law's house, where she died.

Notes

[1] The original pagination of the *History of Orange* is incorrect, as The Middle Years section page should be page 67. The printer apparently forgot to account for this page and its verso.

[2] The Alling mills remained in the Jerusalem section of Orange until 1858, not 1759, as Woodruff states.

Tragedy Strikes The Town

PART IV.

TRAGEDY STRIKES THE TOWN

THE year 1859 was a dark and tragic one for Orange. In the Connecticut Medical Society Proceedings, 1858-1863, we find this item: "Within the past four years, diphtheria has been unusually prevalent. In 1858-9 it made its appearance in many parts of the United States, especially in New York, Massachusetts and Connecticut; prevailing both as an epidemic and sporadically." It struck Orange in March, 1859. The story of it is best told by the editorials which appeared in the New Haven papers of that time.

New Haven Palladium, Friday, April 8, 1859

A STRANGE DISEASE

"A remarkable epidemic which has puzzled our most skillful physicians has made its appearance in Orange, and has caused great consternation, there. It has already caused the death of eight persons, and two others are beyond hope of recovery, if indeed they have not died, today. Drs. Chas. Hooker, Ives and Knight of this city, and Daggett, Beardsley and Dutton of Milford have been called; and they say they have never seen anything of the sort, and do not know what to call the disease, and are utterly at a loss to know what treatment should be adopted. The attack commences with a sore throat, which soon assumes a form of most malignant ulceration, finally the throat swells unaccountably, and the sufferer dies. The physicians say the disease is not like the ordinary, ulcerated sore throat, nor like the 'black tongue,' but exhibits features different from any disease on record.

"Nearly all that have been taken thus far have died, and in some cases its progress is fearfully rapid, though death is usually delayed from a week to two weeks after the first seizure. Most of those who have been attacked thus far have been children, and the full malignity of the disease is not exhibited in the case of adults. Two children have died in one day, this week, and in some families, three or four have been stricken down by this strange malady."

We quote from the *New Haven Journal-Courier*, Monday, April 11, 1859: "More deaths in Orange. Two children, one a daughter of Merwin Andrew, aged seven years; and the other a daughter of Isaac Porter, aged eight years, died in Orange, yesterday, adding two more victims to the malignant throat disease which is now prevailing to an alarming extent in that town. Mr. Andrew, we understand, has lost four and Mr. Porter, three children by the same disease within a short period of time."

Both the *Palladium* of Tuesday, April 12, and the *Journal-Courier* of Wednesday, April 13, 1859, carried this article, entitled "The Orange Malady":

"Messrs. Editors,—I send you the following deaths in Orange. April 10, J. Dwight, only child of Merwin and Elizabeth Andrew, aged seven years. This is the fourth and only child of Mr. Andrew; they have all died of the strange disease that is raging in Orange within two weeks. April 10, Charles, son of Isaac and Phebe Porter, aged eight years. April 10, Phebe Porter, wife of Isaac Porter, aged 36 years. This leaves Mr. Porter a widower and childless, having lost his three children and his wife, in one week. April 12, Collin B., son of Dennis B. and Sarah A. Stone, aged 11 years. There are a number sick here, now. All have died that have been sick, thus far. Many have left town; and all the children are taken away that are well enough to go."

Every one was so frightened that it was difficult to find any one who had courage enough to go into the stricken homes to help bury the dead. Alpheus Merwin and Stiles D. Woodruff dared to do it, so they assisted in most of the burials.

From the Vital Statistics, town of Orange, for the year 1859, we take the following list:

Name	Month	Age	Mo.	Cause
Nancy M. Sheldon	Mch. 18	15		diphtheria
Charles M. Andrew	" 23	4	3	"
Howard Raymond	" 30	10		"
Nelson S. Andrew	Apr. 2	2	4	"
Isaac B. Porter	" 2	15	2	"
Frank N. Andrew	" 4	8	9	"
Alice Porter	" 7	11	3	"
Emerson H. Treat	" 7	11		"
Elizabeth Beardsley	" 9	15		"
J. Dwight Andrew	" 10	7		"
Charles Porter	" 10	7	10	"
Phebe Porter	" 11	36	5	"
Collin B. Stone	" 11	10		"
Ellen M. Stone	" 14	22		"
Frank DeWitt Bradley	May 10	3		"

To offset this awful tale of infant mortality, the town gradually recovered and was even advertised as a health resort. We offer an article appearing in the *New Haven Morning Palladium*, during the year 1874, to substantiate this statement.

ORANGE

"The following facts may serve to show that the length of life to which many in the Orange parish have attained cannot well be surpassed, and that Orange is a good place to live in. During the year 1873, eleven persons died; the youngest was seventy-one, the eldest ninety-five. How is that for long life? With an elevation of more than two hundred feet above tide water, removed largely from that chilliness incident to a nearness to the sea, blessed with pure air, good water, dry localities and pleasant surroundings, with a good high school, a daily mail, a neat and commodious church, and every means for improvement, health, happiness and long life, in the midst of good society, what place can be more conducive to or desirable for a protracted stay in the world than this?

"Already the change wrought by the advent of the steam cars is a wonder to all. Previous to that event, not a *Daily Palladium* paid its morning visit to add zest to the breakfast table; now it finds its way into many households, a welcome messenger. Land has been laid out into lots, and several houses are in process of erection, and steps have already been taken to put up more. Everything goes to show that in Orange you may live long, and with the blessing of Providence, live well."

Before anyone had even dreamt of an automobile or an improved road, let alone a Parkway, there was a little road starting at the Grassy Hill Road, crossing Turkey Hill Road, and extending as far as the Derby-Milford Road. This was called Cranberry Lane, and there was one house on it, a typical Colonial house built by David Treat. His son, David, succeeded him. He was a bachelor, and was the last of his family line. He always kept a diary, as well as a daily account book. His farm was small and did not require all of his time, so he often worked by the day for some of his neighbors. From his daily account book, we have taken a few items, showing the scale of wages paid him in the year 1852. The price seemed to vary according to the work:

1852.

Jan.	26, to 1 days work at wood	$.50
Feb.	4 " " " " " "	.50
Feb.	13 " " " " threshing oats	.50
Apr.	2 " " " " ploughing & cleaning meadow	.50
July	3 " " " " raking & binding rye	.87
July	31 " " " " at hay	.87
Aug.	2 " " " " " "	.87
Aug.	31 " " " " " salt hay	.75
Oct.	22 " " " " digging potatoes	.75
Nov.	11 " " " " picking corn	.75

This shows the daily remuneration received by the ordinary day worker, about one hundred years ago.

Resuming the story of the Orange Congregational Church, we find that at a meeting of the Ecclesiastical

Society held December 2, 1844, they were progressive enough to vote to purchase a stove for burning coal, but evidently this was not a popular vote, for later the subject was brought up again, the vote to buy a coal stove was rescinded, and they proceeded to auction off the furnishing of the year's supply of wood to the lowest bidder. This had to be good quality hickory wood, seasoned, cut, and split ready for the two stoves. It was bid off for seven dollars per cord. The first cabinet organ was purchased in the Fall of 1863. After the service held on Sunday, January 17, 1864, the church was closed, to begin extensive alterations. The old high pulpit was removed and the seating arrangement changed; the entire cost of the alterations was $3650. The opening service of rededication was held June 9, 1864.

The oldest society maintained by the women of the Church was the Orange Auxiliary of the New Haven Branch of the Woman's Board for Foreign Missions, organized May 4, 1877. Other organizations were the Auxiliary of the Woman's Home Missionary Union of Connecticut. The Ladies Benevolent Society was organized December 12, 1883.

The year 1886 was an eventful year for the Church, for during that year a new pipe organ was purchased, and a new furnace was installed, doing away with the two stoves with their long pipes extending the length of the church on each side aisle.

One of the causes of annoyance at church services, particularly in summer when the doors and windows were open, was the geese. Probably every family living near the church and Green kept a flock. The separate flocks used the Green for a common rendezvous, and when they met, there was apt to be a great squawking and cackling, sometimes drowning out the preacher's words. Not even the tithingman's staff could exercise any authority in that case.

Between the morning and afternoon services there was quite a long interval, during which the people had time to eat their lunches and could meet in groups and gossip together. In summer the men sat on the long steps extending on three sides of the steeple and talked about the crops and about their weekly experiences. The value of this feature of the church service can hardly be over-rated. Through these gatherings the men and women became intimately acquainted with one another, without which opportunity they would have known little about their fellow townsmen. They had no telephones nor a daily paper. These gatherings at the country churches throughout New England and in other parts of the land, while they may not have furnished much spiritual edification, did nevertheless materially contribute to the social side of life. Of course there were some each Sunday who attended only one service and so lost the benefit of the intermission.

The question has often been asked: "How did the people manage to live and support the large families which were quite common in the early days?" They raised few crops that were sold for cash; most of what they grew was consumed on the premises. We are told that most of their transactions were by way of exchange, so that they needed little actual cash. Butter, cheese, and poultry were staple products, but the results from these sources were not great. Probably livestock was their most de-pendable source of income, especially during the years immediately following the Civil War. Prices for cattle were high, and a trim pair of working oxen could be sold for $325. Older ones which were turned off for beef brought good prices, so that the shrinkage in value on cattle which were kept for a period of years was com-paratively small, while the horse, after he had outlived his usefulness, became a dead loss. Goose-raising was also a side line of some importance, and nearly every family in the country kept a flock. The goose had value, whether living or dead. Like sheep-shearing, goose-plucking from both live or dead birds was a common practice.

Goose-feather beds were considered indispensable in every well-ordered household, and were costly.

A popular song of the early days ran like this:

"Go tell Aunt Rhoda,
Go tell Aunt Rhoda,
Go tell Aunt Rhoda
The old gray goose is dead.

She's worth a saving,
She's worth a saving,
She's worth a saving
To make a featherbed."

Of course the fox was the natural enemy of the goose. The goose was a natural wanderer, and sometimes the flock would stray far afield, so far that the owner could not find it convenient to look up the flock and drive it back to the fold at night; and as the goose roosts on the ground, Sir Fox would have his opportunity. The most efficient method for limiting the foxes was to dig out their burrows in the Spring, when they had their young.

Hog raising was also an important side line. To grow up a pen of fat hogs was the ambition of the average farmer. Pigs that had been kept over the previous winter were often made to weigh 400 pounds, dressed weight. Then during a cold snap in the early winter, the important day of hog-killing arrived. Not only weather conditions had to be considered, but the right phase of the moon must be selected, otherwise the pork from pigs killed in the "old of the moon" would shrink in the pot.

Soon after the hog-killing day came the time for making sausages. Bacon was not used so much, so those cuts which would now be put into bacon were put into sausages, with some beef added. The solid fat portions of the hog, of course, became the "salt pork," and the pork barrel was an established institution. To salt down a barrel of pork, and properly cure and smoke the hams and shoulders so that they would keep "sweet" throughout the year, required skill and patience.

85

Not only for a supply of pork but also for beef the farmer provided. During the Winter time a quarter or more of beef could be hung up to freeze and be used when needed; but for Summer use the meat had to be packed in barrels and properly covered with brine, correctly prepared.

"Sheep-washing" day was a welcome treat for the boys, as they could get into the water and have a good time under the guise of being at work. It was also very satisfactory to be able to take some stiff necked "old buck" by the horns and give him a good ducking, head and eyes under, who was so fearless and hard to manage when on land. The shearing time came soon after, and the great, white fleeces, tied up in sheets, were carried to the house, ready for carding into rolls for spinning.

In Winter the attics of these old houses were filled with all kinds of aromas. Strings of apples were hung up on nails to dry; many kinds of medicinal herbs were carefully dried—bags of hops, bunches of thyme, savory sage and fennel; boneset and penny-royal; peppermint, wormwood, and wintergreen; roots of sassafras and sarsaparilla.

The cider mill was an established institution in the earlier days. They were to be found on many farms. The building was four-square, inclosing a large, circular trough, through which, after the apples had been deposited a very large wooden wheel was drawn by a horse until the apples were thoroughly crushed. The pomace was then pressed under very large and skillfully constructed screws, which were turned down, from time to time, as the juice oozed out. As the pressure was more effectual near the center of the mass than on the edges, before bedtime it was necessary to cut down the edges of the "cheese," reconstruct the formation and set the screws for the night. How a profitable market could have been obtained for the product of all these cider mills is hard to understand. Some of it was allowed to age until it became vinegar, but much of it was used as a beverage, either sweet or "hard" cider.

Candles were also home made. One important day in each year was candle-dipping day. These had all to be dipped by hand, a long and tedious process. Later molds were produced, which helped to shorten the task.

Another essential commodity found in each household was the barrel of soft soap. This was made by the house-wife, would last for a long time, and was used for all ordinary cleaning purposes.

In a manuscript entitled "History of the Old, Red House," written by Henry L. Woodruff in 1884, we are given a description of an early farm house and the buildings which made up the complete outfit. This house stood at the corner of Old Tavern Road and Lambert Road. It was built about 1775 by Matthew Woodruff, and was destroyed by fire on July 10, 1883. The cellar hole may still be found on the southwest corner of Corbin's hill.

"Directly south across the road stood the gigantic barn, of unknown age, surrounded on three sides by the necessary out buildings. A little to the east, and on the rise of the knoll, on a line with the house, stood the massive two story cider-mill, and just beyond, in a little depression, under the shelter of the hill, was the flax mill. Altogether a group of farm buildings, which for style, convenience, and amplitude, were not excelled by any in town. The red house was forty feet front and thirty-two feet, rear, with a chimney twelve by thirteen feet square The barn was undoubtedly much older than the house. It was said that the timber was cut from the forest immediately adjoining and that the settlers came up from Milford, bringing their rifles with them as a means of defense against the Indians, while they were at work.

"Nearly every farm included the cultivation of flax, which was a necessity in the manufacture of cloth. When it was fully ripe, the flax was pulled up by the roots and spread thinly and evenly in rows on the ground, and thus left exposed for some weeks in order to rot the central woody stalk, so that it could be broken up and separated from the back, or fibre. Then it was gathered into bundles and carried to the flax house, where was the rude, special machinery for preparing it for spinning. After going through the process of the breaker, the swingle and the hatchel, until the proper degree of cleanness and fineness is secured. It was then twisted, doubled in the center, and secured with a band of the same, and in huge baskets, carried to the home, ready for the spinning wheel."

The Tinder Box

There were no matches in the early days, and to light a fire or a candle was a difficult problem. So the tinder box was a household treasure. This was a tin box, about four inches in diameter, filled with tinder, with a close fitting cover on the inside. To prepare this tinder, a piece of old cotton cloth was burned, and when all a live coal, placed in the box and then extinguished by pressing down the cover. This tinder was highly inflammable. To ignite it, a steel curved like a horse-shoe magnet was held by the left hand over the open box and struck with the flint, held in the right hand. A spark rolled off, and touching the tinder, ignited it instantly. Then a "loco-foco" or Lucifer match being applied, it kindled the brimstone, burning with a bluish yellow flame, by which a fire could be started or a candle lighted. This Lucifer match was simply a thin shaving of white pine, dipped on one end in melted brimstone, and was ignited by contact with the fire. As the morning fire could be more readily kindled with the warm live embers, it was the custom to cover them carefully on retiring at night. But if they failed, the tinder box had to be relied on in the emergency. And if this method failed to bring results, it meant that some one would have to go to the nearest neighbor's to borrow some live coals.

Modes of Travel

During the years after the settlement of the town and well into the nineteenth century, the roads were not good, and much of the travel was on horseback. Many of these roads or trails ran over steep hills and ledges, and many such roads have since been abandoned. In the layout of the roads more attention seems to have been paid to the preservation of rectangular fields than to the convenience of travel. It is believed that in those earlier years men were more occupied with their daily pursuits than in travelling about, and when they did have occasion to go, they often went on foot, or "across lots." The result of this scheme of transportation was to run the roads over steep hills, when the same distance would have taken the road around the hill, nearly on the level. Even the Turnpikes, the building of which was commenced after the close of the Revolutionary War and carried on well into the nineteenth century, seem to have been constructed on much the same plan as the common roads. The difficulties of obtaining rights of way for a new road were undoubtedly very real in the olden days, just as much as they are at the present time. The farmers protested stoutly against having their fields and forests "cut into." These early roads were not paved or improved in any way, and the difficulty of travel in the early Spring was very acute.

The vehicles used for travel during the early days were, of course, rather crude and often uncomfortable, although carriage-building made great progress in New Haven during the years preceding the Civil War. It is said that Levi Beecher, who was more prosperous than his neighbors, owned the first carriage in Orange. His death occurred in 1850, and amongst the buildings inventoried in his estate was a carriage house.

The other Orange people rode in such go-carts as they could afford. This was especially true of those vehicles which moved on runners. Pungs and contraptions of almost any construction were thought good enough to travel through the snow. It may be doubted whether the stage-coach, with all the classical distinction that has been accorded to it, was an altogether comfortable conveyance when hurried over the rough roads of those early days at the speed it was supposed to travel.

OCCUPATIONS AND TRADES

While the citizens were primarily farmers, there were also representatives of other industries. In the "horse and buggy" days, both the horse and the buggy sometimes needed the attention of a blacksmith, so his indispensable shop was a necessity. The earliest one of which we can find record was maintained by Henry Russell, at the northeast corner of the Derby Turnpike and Race Brook Road. After he returned from the Civil War, Stephen Russell opened a blacksmith's shop on the Derby Turnpike, just east of Race Brook Road. He continued this business for many years; he also made wagons. His property was later sold to Howard Stevens, who was a building contractor.

On the Milford Turnpike, Shaw's blacksmith shop took care of the needs of the horses in that part of the town. Another blacksmith shop was on Orange Center Road, directly back of Mr. Miller's Grocery Store, where the abandoned building still stands. Fred Wheeler, living in the house now occupied by George T. Hine, was a carpenter and building contractor. Another carpenter and builder was Lyman Nettleton, whose place later became the home of Wilson H. Lee. Mr. Nettleton was a dreamer. He used to say that some day people would fly through the air, and that the day would come when people could make daily trips to Europe. His ideas were so fantastic that his contemporaries considered him a bit unbalanced. They did not realize that he was a prophet.

Eli Elvington was an expert mason, whose services were in great demand. His former home was demolished to make room for the Wilbur Cross Parkway.

Another very necessary trade was that of shoemaker, and there were several who followed this trade. Some of them went around to the homes, outfitting the whole family while there. Usually, however, they had a little shop at their homes. Some of the men who made shoes were William Ell Russell, on Race Brook Road; William Grant, who lived at the Green; Ellsworth Foote, who

90

lived in the Boppert place; Sidney Oviatt, and Benjamin Somers. In the early days of the town, men usually wore boots. The ordinary price of these hand-made shoes was about two dollars. Another who learned the shoemaker's trade was Albert Miles. He was the son of Captain Daniel Miles, who was lost at sea during the war of 1812, while bringing in a captive vessel. Albert was a very young boy when his father died, and came to live with Mr. and Mrs. Edmund Fowler on Orange Center Road. In his "Register of the Inhabitants of North Milford," Mr. Scranton lists Albert Miles as the adopted son of Mr. and Mrs. Fowler. At any rate, they left him their property. His old house is an interesting type of early architecture, and is now owned by John W. Gamsby.

There was a factory where checker boards were made, which was located on the Derby Turnpike, near the present Daisy Hill Gardens. Still another type of trade was followed by Wm. Chauncey Russell, that of selling both retail and wholesale meat. He had a meat route through Orange. He combined his efforts, for when in New Haven to get his supply of meat, he also collected the mail at the New Haven Post Office and delivered it to Sidney Oviatt's home. The Orange Post Office was maintained there for some time. Later, when the New Haven and Derby Railroad was started, Mr. Oviatt became the station agent, so then the Post Office was moved down to the railroad station.

The women of the town were mostly modest, retiring, busy housekeepers; but there was one outstanding exception. Miss Emily Prudden was a direct descendant of Rev. Peter Prudden, the head of the Milford Colony. After bringing up the children of a sister who died in early life, Miss Prudden looked around for other fields of endeavor. Well into middle life, and with the added handicap of almost total deafness, she decided to try to help the poor mountaineers of North Carolina to get a little education.

With her own meager funds, she would seek out a neglected area and there build and equip a school. The outfit was crude, but with determination, she would get

91

started. Then, when she had managed to get it in running order, she would turn that school over to some Mission Board and look around for a new field. Her judgment in selecting sites was excellent, for three of the schools which she turned over to the American Missionary Association have developed into famous institutions: Skyland Institute at Blowing Rock, Lincoln Academy at King's Mountain, and Saluda Seminary at Saluda.

Fifteen such schools or colleges stand to her credit. She chose to live out her days among the people she loved, and died in North Carolina on Christmas Day, 1917, at the age of 85. At her request, she was brought home to her native town for burial.

Since oxen were used quite extensively on the farms, Elbee J. Treat developed quite a thriving business by bringing oxen from Guilford and other eastern towns and selling them locally. The same line of business was carried on by George T. Hine and later by his son, Walter S. Hine. He dealt in both oxen and cows. Mr. Hine first obtained his animals from Vermont, then later from Liberty, in Sullivan County, New York. He would bring them by the carload, selling them at public auction. Sometimes the auctions were held in Orange, but usually they were held in Newtown, Conn.

Another important business which has been conducted for years has been the growing of garden and field seeds for the wholesale market. This business was started in the town of Derby by a Mr. Hodge, who then sold out his interests to two brothers in Orange, Enoch and Bryan Clark. In 1864, Everett B. Clark succeeded his father, Bryan Clark, and enlarged the scope of the business. He grew seeds on his own farm, also engaged farmers to grow seeds for him. His farms were in Orange, but his business headquarters was in Milford. As his sons grew older, he took them into the business with him. After the death of Everett B. Clark, the sons continued the business, until eventually they merged with some other seed companies, calling it the Associated Seed Growers, and moved their main office to New Haven.

The same line of growing and selling seeds was carried on by Stiles D. Woodruff. After his return from the Civil War, he bought the farm of Lyman Treat and immediately began to grow seeds for the wholesale trade. In 1890 he took his sons, Frank C. and Watson S., into the business with him, under the firm name of S. D. Woodruff & Sons. They opened a branch store in New York City, under the management of Frank C. Woodruff, while Watson S. Woodruff had charge of the home office. On the death of their father in 1906, the two brothers continued the business until the death of Watson S. in 1930, when Frank C. managed to carry on alone. In 1944, just prior to his death, he sold his interests in the business to Hugh C. Laird and Eric Dahlberg, who still maintain the business under the original name of S. D. Woodruff & Sons.

For many, many years there has been a general store in the town. The early records show that John Bryan had a store near the Green. Later a store was run by George M. White in the building just across the street from the railroad station and the Post Office. In 1883 Mr. White sold his interests in the store to two brothers from New Haven, William J. and George W. Scobie. This firm existed for a couple of years, when the business was assumed by William J. Scobie. Later Elbert W. Scobie joined his father, eventually succeeding him in the business. In 1925 a new building was constructed just a few rods south and across the street from the cemetery, and Mr. Scobie moved the store there. In 1938 the store was taken over by Irving Miller, the present manager.

THE POST OFFICE

In the early days of the town, the Post Office was located near the Green. Previous to 1861, postmasters were William T. Grant, Benjamin T. Clark, and Dennis B. Stone. Later Sidney F. Oviatt maintained the Post Office in his home just south of the Green. When the Derby-New Haven Railroad was opened in 1871, Mr. Oviatt

93

became the first station agent, and the Post Office was moved down to the railroad station.

On the death of Mr. Oviatt in 1888, William J. Scobie was appointed Postmaster, and the Post Office was moved across the street to the general store. When the new store was built across from the cemetery, Mr. Scobie moved the Post Office there also. Eventually Elbert Scobie became Postmaster, being succeeded in that position in 1935 by William J. Rourke. On January 1, 1938, after the death of Mr. Rourke, Raymond Cuzzocreo became Postmaster, which position he now holds.

In 1943 the Post Office moved to larger quarters, occupying the front of the warehouse owned by Frank C. Woodruff. As the town continued to grow and the volume of mail became greater, the Post Office demanded even more space, so on January 1, 1949, it was moved into a new brick building which had been built for that purpose by Mrs. Maurice Rogers—an attractive and appropriate building well suited to its needs.

Rural Free Delivery was inaugurated in Orange in 1902, and on July 1, Albert M. Clark made his first trip as the rural mail carrier. He received hearty greetings all along the way. When he reached Grassy Hill, Carleton Woodruff came out with his gun and fired off a welcoming salute. Through rain or snow, Mr. Clark continued to deliver the mail for over thirty-three years. Mrs. William Rourke followed him for a few years, until her place was taken in 1938 by Henry Peterson. In 1941 the route was taken over by John Kowal. Because of the growth of the town, two routes were established in 1949. The area was extended to include the Boston Post Road, which had formerly been covered from West Haven. Route No. 1 is covered by Edward Ciola, while John Kowal continues to serve Route No. 2.

The change wrought by the passage of almost fifty years is noteworthy: Mr. Clark began with sixty-one families; the two routes now serve seven hundred boxes, or eight hundred and seventy-five families.

The busy housewife did not have to go to the city

THE FIRST RURAL MAIL OUTFIT

THE FIRST POST OFFICE AND SCOBIE'S STORE[1]

THE NEW POST OFFICE

—*Photo by Jonathan Rogers*

for all her needs; some of them came right to her door. One of the traveling merchants was the "tin-peddler." His wagon was unique, being hung on straps instead of springs. The tin-peddler carried everything in the tin line that could possibly be put on or in, or hung on or under, the vehicle. He bartered with all the women along the routes, who saved their rags and feathers to trade for useful articles. Then there were the "pack-peddlers," who arrived with staggering loads on their backs and, if they could gain a foothold over the threshold, spread out their goods on the floor of the living room and did their best to persuade the family to buy their wares.

Other callers at the back door, not to sell but to beg for food, were the tramps. For more than two hundred years in the Connecticut Colony there had been laws concerning vagrancy, and the several counties had been required to maintain workhouses for the confinement of vagabonds. This provision was later modified so as to allow each county to determine for itself whether it would provide workhouses; and it was further provided that no one should be confined without due process of law. For many years the interpretation of this had been to let the tramp alone, unless he had been guilty of some criminal act. So some of them roamed the streets and begged for food.

The most notorious of these tramps, who made his rounds more or less systematically, was the "old leather man." He was a mystery whose secret no one was ever able to discover. He won his name because of his outfit: his suit was made up entirely of old boot tops or other scraps of leather, stitched together. These garments created a rattle when he walked, and naturally the dogs took offence to him. On his back he carried a pack which contained pieces of leather with which to mend his suit. He would suddenly appear in town, going south to Milford, always following the same route and stopping at the same houses. He spent his nights in caves or sheltered places. He was believed to be a French Canadian, since he could not converse with people, and some tried to add a touch of romance to his story, but no one ever found out his real identity or history.

The authorities of Hamden had him committed to the Asylum at Middletown, but he made his escape, and when last seen in Danbury, he appeared very feeble, as he was suffering from a cancer of the lip. In the *New Haven Register* of March 24, 1889, is an account of his death. He was found lying dead in a cave at Mt. Pleasant, near Sing Sing, New York.[2]

Notes

[1] The first post office was established in Orange in 1844 with Philo N. Curtis as the first postmaster. The post office was discontinued the following year and re-established in 1854 with Dennis B. Stone as postmaster.

[2] Woodruff's assessment of "The Leatherman" is in keeping with both her times and social prominence. While much has been written of "The Old Leatherman" and the 365-mile circuitous route he trekked on his way through at least 41 towns in Connecticut and New York every 34 days from 1883 until his death in 1889, his true identity remains unknown, according to Dan DeLuca, the author of *The Old Leather Man (2008)*. He is buried in Sparta Cemetery, just south of Ossining, New York. His headstone reads "Jules Bourglay," purportedly his real name. That, however, has since proven to be unfounded.

The Bubble That Burst

PART V.

THE TYLER CITY BUBBLE

THE railroad between New Haven and Derby was under construction from 1867 to 1871 and was put into operation on August 5, 1871. Older residents recall that there were six trains in either direction every week day.[1] This led to the belief that all the land adjacent to the railroad would be in demand for business or residential purposes.

Two New Haven prospectors, Messrs. Philander Ferry and Samuel Halliwell, followed the course of the railroad, seeking a new town site. The farm of Lewis Bradley took their eye. This was claimed to be one of the best farms in Orange, consisting of about one hundred and seventy-five acres. They added to that some land belonging to Mr. Ell Russell. They bought this land, thinking that it would be the beginning of a new metropolis, and as it was adjacent to the new railroad, they called it Tyler City, after the President of the railroad, Morris Tyler.

On the 14th of March, 1872, a few avenues were cut among the trees and the foundations laid for two luxurious mansions. This land was first cleared by cutting down the trees and making charcoal pits by piling up the wood.

To get the trains to stop at Tyler City, the hopeful realtors built a two-story station and presented it to the railroad. Although this building was accepted, Tyler City was always just a flag stop on the line.[2] The following advertisement appeared in one of the New Haven papers: "For sale, 2000 building lots in Tyler City, the best and cheapest in New Haven County. Only twelve minutes from New Haven on the Derby railroad. A free ticket will be given for one year to the head of every family who buys this Spring." "Notice: Those taking up their residence in Tyler City will be on the main road for New York and the West, and cannot help realizing in the future by buying now."

A public auction was held on July 10, 1872, and people came to Tyler City by carriage, by cart, on foot, and by train. When the flurry of buying had ceased, the proprietors had increased their capital by $510,000.[3] Mr. Ferry, who owned a large bakery in New Haven, completed his elaborate house in a short time, and his grounds were handsomely landscaped.

As time passed, the hopes of a great metropolis dwindled. Notes were allowed to lapse, and the property returned to the realtors.

At the corner of Ferry Avenue and Crofut Street Mr. Edwin Robbins built a large house, in which he started to conduct a boarding school for boys, which he called "Altworth Hall." A folder, printed in 1878, advertised it as a preparatory school for business or for college entrance requirements. It was never successful, and continued only a few years. Later this same building was occupied by the recently formed New Haven County Children's Home. A request was made of the Town to build sidewalks from the Home to the railroad station, and when this petition was not granted, the Home was moved nearer New Haven.[4]

The Halliwell residence was never fully completed as originally planned. Some years later, it was used as a club room for the Orange Hunt Club. At the present time, the property is used by the Orange Riding Stables.

The Tyler City school district was formed in 1873. During the first year (1873-74) the school was held in one of the two waiting rooms of the railroad station. When the fall term opened on September 1, 1874, it was held in the new schoolhouse which was just completed.

A Post Office was established in Tyler City, which was run by Charles Amesbury, in his house located across the street from the railroad station. He also conducted a grocery store and lived upstairs over the store.

A factory was built near the station, beside the railroad tracks. About 1871, The Sackett Manufacturing Company started business there, but soon failed. Afterward, in 1887, the premises were taken over by the Peerless Buttonhole Attachment Company, Inc.[5] J. Willis Downes of New Haven and William Chauncey Russell of Tyler City were the business partners, Mr. Downes being the Treasurer. This likewise proved unprofitable, so it was discontinued. Using the basement of the building, Edward W. Russell conducted a creamery, where he made butter which was sold both wholesale and retail. In 1897, business was resumed here by a company which made tricycles and baby-carriages. Unfortunately, just before the Christmas season, when the building was full of holiday goods ready for shipment, it caught fire and was totally destroyed.

Near the railroad station, a man started making plaster-of-Paris centerpieces, used to decorate ceilings. He made very ornate ones which were used in the Ferry and Halliwell houses, and he started to build a factory to go into the business in a larger way, but he never got beyond the foundation of his building.

Across the railroad track at Tyler City there was a very fine grove, which made an ideal place for picnic parties and other gatherings. Some of these gatherings were addressed by prominent citizens, such as the Governor of the State, the Mayor of New Haven, and others. One frequent visitor was George Beckwith, the author of the famous Almanac. He was somewhat eccentric, and his usual costume was a long tail-coat and white beaver hat. He was always barefooted. Being a very interesting speaker, he was eagerly welcomed. Later this grove was used by a group of colored people as a Camp-meeting ground.[6]

Mention was previously made of David Treat, who lived on Cranberry Lane, and of his custom of always keeping a diary. From one volume of his diary we quote the entry for Saturday, November 4, 1882. This item would be an every-day occurrence in the present age, but sixty years ago it shocked the town. Mr. Treat had retired about ten o'clock. Shortly afterwards, he was aroused by loud knocking at both the front and back doors. On answering the summons, he was told that it was a United States detective looking for a man, with a warrant to search the house, and demanding to be admitted. When he opened the door, four masked men rushed in, pointing pistols and telling him to hold up his hands. They then said, "Money or your life." He was forced to comply, and going to a chest, Mr. Treat produced two pocket books containing $15.50, every cent he had in the house. Not satisfied with the amount, the ruffians knocked him down and tortured and abused him shamefully and disgracefully. Finally, after wrecking the house, they left, warning him that if he gave any alarm before they had time to escape, he would be shot. The next day he managed to make his way to the home of Stiles D. Woodruff, his conservator, to relate his experience. That allowed the culprits plenty of time to get away. However, through some clever detective work on the part of the conservator, all four young men, residents of Derby, were eventually apprehended and convicted. They served six years in State's Prison for their crime.

By 1873 West Haven had become more than a village and felt that the rural town government was not adequate to their needs of better roads, street lighting, police and fire protection.

The Borough of West Haven was, therefore, created by the General Assembly in May, 1873. The Selectmen continued at the head of the town government, but the Borough was administered by a Warden and a Board of Burgesses. Taxes were levied by both the Town and the Borough.

There were frequent controversies between the "upper section" and those living in the Borough. The citizens of the farming section wanted to keep their government simple and as inexpensive as possible, while the Borough advocated higher taxes in order to obtain the improvements they felt they needed.[7]

At a Town Meeting held on July 24, 1862, it was voted "that each recruit who may enlist as volunteer soldiers shall be paid $100 from the town treasury on being sworn into service." This amount was increased on September 5 to $200, to fill the quota asked of the Town.

On October 6, 1873, they voted that a high school should be established in Orange, but there was a delay of five years before this was an accomplished fact.

At this same Town Meeting, a committee was also appointed, consisting of the Selectmen, Samuel L. Smith and Benjamin T. Clark, to consider the purchase of the stock of the Milford Turnpike Company. On October 4, 1875, this purchasing committee was enlarged by adding three more to assist them: George T. Hine, J. Sheldon Alling, and Stephen D. Russell. They voted to buy the stock, provided that it could be acquired at a sum not exceeding $30 per share. On October 1, 1877, the Town voted to instruct the Selectmen to provide a new hearse for the use of the Town of Orange.

At a town meeting, October 7, 1878, it was voted "that the sum of $1500 be taken from the Treasury and used to erect a building at Orange Center for high school and public purposes."

A special Town Meeting held on August 4, 1881, records the following action: "Voted that the town offer a bounty of $300 for detection and conviction of any person stealing a horse from any citizen of the town of Orange, $100 for stealing a carriage or wagon, and $25 for stealing a harness."

The first mention of a public celebration of Memorial Day is found in the action taken at a Town Meeting on October 3, 1887, when it was voted "that $50 be appropriated for the expense of Decoration Day; $30 to the West Haven Memorial Association, $20 to Elizur B. Russell, for Orange."

After the Town Hall and schoolhouse were built at the Center, Town Meetings were held there rather than at the little town building built down on the Turnpike. This building had stood idle for years, so at a Town Meeting on October 1, 1894, it was voted "to appoint an auctioneer to sell the old town hall on the Milford Turnpike to the highest bidder."

Charles F. Smith was appointed, and the building was sold to Thomas Mills for $48.

Much has been written and sung about the "Gay Nineties." The young people of Orange were gay and had a good time during the seventies or eighties. Distance did not seem to hinder them, and if the means of transportation was slow, that did not bother them, either. Sometimes they would join a group from Milford for a dance, or they might go to Woodbridge; but wherever they went, Mr. John Anthony was sure to be on hand with his violin. His enthusiasm, as he fiddled and called off the figures for the square dances, was caught by all the dancers. Mr. Anthony's vocation during the day was to go around to the houses selling bluing, essences, and candy. Winter's cold did not worry the younger set, and if the trip should include a sleigh ride, so much the better. Sometimes it was a barn dance, with a husking bee to give the added interest.

About this period, two acts of Nature had a very disastrous effect on the community. On May 29, 1884, there was such a heavy frost that it killed every growing thing —all the fruit, the vegetables, and the flowers. It was such a calamity that for years afterwards people talked about "the great freeze."

Then in March, 1888, occurred the big blizzard. It began to snow on Sunday afternoon, March 12, and the snow continued to fall for three days and nights. On Monday morning, the district schools did not open, but a few hardy girls and boys braved the storm and went to the High School on the Green. Although the school closed at noon, by that time the storm was so severe that the children could not reach their homes, but stopped to spend the night with some kind neighbor, who lived near the Green. Having no telephones to ascertain their whereabouts, the parents had to hope and pray they were safe.

A combination three-car freight and passenger train started from Derby at 7 A.M. to go to New Haven, with thirteen passengers. They were stuck in the drifts when they reached the cut at Platt Valley. All that day, and throughout Monday night, they were marooned on the train. By Tuesday afternoon, the group climbed through the drifts to the nearest farm house. Fortunately for the passengers, the freight car was carrying six hundred pies, five gallons of oysters, and three hundred pounds of pork, bacon, and sausages. Six of the group remained at the house; the others returned to the train. By Wednesday the brakeman and five other men managed to make their way to New Haven, and on Thursday a rescue party came to take away the rest of the weary travelers. One hundred men dug for four days to open a path to New Haven, so that milk could be delivered to that needy city. The opening in the drifts was made just wide enough for a sleigh or a farm-sled to get through.

Nearly a month later, on April 7, occurred the death of one of the older residents, who lived in the Turkey Hill section. A force of men had to dig for two days in order to widen the roads to allow the passage of the hearse and the funeral carriages. Some traces of the snow were still to be found in the month of May.

In 1934, about February 22, it began to look as if history was going to repeat itself; but the snow stopped after two days, and while the drifts were high, they could not be compared with the blizzard of 1888. The present system of snow plows, constantly keeping the main roads open, helped people to get around more readily.

THE PLUMED KNIGHTS

During the political campaign of 1884, when James G. Blaine was the Republican candidate for the Presidency, the young men of the Town formed a mounted troop to

107

Orange Green

- Photo by Jonathan Rodgers

assist in torch light parades. They called themselves the "Plumed Knights." Their mounts were not fancy polo ponies—just their faithful farm horses; but as they were the only mounted troop in this section of the County, they were in great demand, and created quite a sensation whenever they visited the surrounding towns or cities. They had distinctive uniforms, and each man carried a lighted torch. They received many invitations to participate in parades.

LANDSCAPING THE GREEN

While the Green was set aside as public property, it was sadly neglected. The old custom of pasturing geese on it had long since been discontinued. The boys had used it as a ball field, but it was no improvement to the town.

In the Fall of 1890 public sentiment began to point toward village improvement. Many public meetings were held and plans discussed, which resulted in vigorous action in the Spring of 1891. The community idea, which has always played such a prominent part in this town, came again into play. The resourceful citizens brought their teams and all worked together, plowing and scraping. Sometimes there were as many as thirty teams at work at the same time. The ground was graded, levelled, and then seeded, to make a central Green of which the Town could be justly proud.

During World War I, a very simple wooden Honor Roll was placed on the northern end of the Green, containing the names of the men and women who were serving their country in various fields. This was only a temporary affair, and a more lasting memorial was considered necessary. Accordingly, a large native boulder was set up, toward the lower end of the Green, with a bronze tablet, suitably inscribed, to commemorate all of the citizens of the town who had answered their country's call in time of war. This was appropriately landscaped and was officially dedicated at the close of the Memorial Exercises on Sunday, May 29, 1932. When World War II again called our boys and girls to the colors, it was felt that their names should occupy a place of prominence, so a very attractive Honor Roll was built around the tall flag-pole in the center of the Green, bearing the names of the hundreds who went to all parts of the world. The dedication of this Honor Roll took place after the Memorial services held on Sunday, May 30, 1943.

The Orange Grange

The Orange Grange, No. 128, was organized at the Town Hall at Orange Center on the evening of December 18, 1891. Its charter roll comprised the following names: Frank C. Woodruff, Stiles D. Woodruff, Henry M. Hunt, Dwight E. Russell, Stephen D. Russell, Elizur B. Russell, Herbert E. Russell, Theron L. Alling, Watson S. Woodruff, Wilbur J. Hoyes, William T. Andrew, Franklin Finney, Julia A. Woodruff, Henry G. Nibbletts, Alice W. Hunt, Mary R. Russell, Anna B. Russell, Ernest Alling, Helena Alling, Charles F. Smith, Bela M. Alling, Mary E. Andrew, and Isabelle Finney. Frank C. Woodruff was elected the first Master.

At the beginning, the meetings were held on the second and fourth Mondays of each month at the Town Hall. Early in 1897 it became manifest that a kitchen and cloak-room would be convenient accessories, and steps were taken towards raising the necessary funds by various methods. On June 18, 1897, a gift was received from the Dorcas Society, which was composed of a group of young ladies of the Town.

A building committee was appointed, and said committee decided not only to build a kitchen and cloakroom, but a hall as well, to be used by the Grange and other organizations. Early in April, 1898, the foundations were laid as an addition to the Town Hall. Arthur D. Clark was the building contractor. As the expense was shared by many who were not members of the Order, the public had joint ownership with the Grange in the new building.

In 1897, through the efforts of the Grange, and the assistance of interested residents, a flag pole was erected

110

on the Green. On September 15, 1898, an agricultural fair was held on the Green, with the following committee in charge: Carleton V. Woodruff, Dwight E. Russell, Frederick J. Treat, and Walter S. Hine. The event netted $150, which was applied to the building fund. The hall had been completed during that summer, at a cost of about $800.

The following year, it was decided that the fair of the previous summer had been so successful that it warranted repetition of the event. September 14 was the day chosen for the fair, which was attended by nearly 5,000 people from neighboring towns. Almost $500 was cleared, so that by November of that year, the Grange Hall was entirely paid for, as well as having some funds left to be used for village improvement.

In 1900, when Dwight E. Russell was Master, the co-operative system of buying grain for feed was used, and seventy-one car loads were bought. By 1902 the membership was one hundred and twenty, with an average attendance of forty-five at the meetings, a strong feature of which was the lecturer's hour. Bela Alling was Master, and the members used the group insurance plan in the Patron's Mutual Fire Insurance Company, amounting to $70,000. The following year, with Walter S. Hine as Master, eighty car loads of feed were bought, and property insured to the value of $100,000.

By 1912 interest in the organization began to wane, although meetings were still being held. Finally, the organization was given up entirely, and those who wanted to continue in the Grange joined with the groups in nearby towns.

Notes

1. George D. Chapman and Co. signed the construction contract on December 30, 1867 and work began shortly thereafter [*Hartford Daily Courant*, January 1, 30, 1868, p. 2]. The state railroad commissioners rode the line on August 4 [*New Haven Daily Palladium*, August 5, 1871, p. 2] and issued a certificate of suitability to operate that allowed two pre-opening excursions on August 5. Regular service began on August 9 with two daily trains each way. [*New Haven Evening Register*, August 8, 1871, p. 2]. These were quickly increased to five [*Register*, September 26, 1871, p. 2], and stayed at about that level, perhaps numbering six briefly, until the Housatonic Railroad took over in 1887.

2. Tyler City was never just a flag stop. It actually saw a dozen or so trains stopping in each direction on weekdays by 1907, probably the peak service level. Only for a brief time in 1879 was there one scheduled stop each way, with the other four trains flagged for waiting passengers.

3. *The Register and New Haven's Daily Morning Journal and Courier* [both, July 3, 1872, p. 2] say the auction was held on July 2. Land records would have to be consulted to verify Woodruff's $510,000 figure, one that seems high but may have included additional sales.

4. The New Haven County Temporary Home for Dependent and Neglected Children debuted on January 1, 1884 in rented space at the former Altworth Hall [*Register*, January 3, 1884, p. 1]. The home later purchased property at Shelton Ave. and Bassett St. in New Haven, to open as of July 1, 1886. [*Register*, June 5, 1886, p. 2]. While sidewalks may have been an issue, a more likely factor in the move was a dispute with the Tyler City school district over accepting the children who were not town residents. [*Courant*, May 19, 1884, p. 4].

5. *The Register* [June 23, 1887, p. 3] says that Sackett was located in Wallingford and just then moving to the Tyler City factory that it later said Halliwell had built [*Register*, November 27, 1888, p. 1]. The corner of this factory is visible in a newspaper photograph [*Register* and *New Haven Journal Courier*, March 14, 1964, p. 8]. The building burned on October 28, 1898 and the last occupant, the New England Tricycle Co., relocated to New Haven [*Courant*, October 29, 1898, p. 13].

6. Woodruff alludes here to a little-known Orange event of great historical significance. Covered repeatedly in the *Register* and elsewhere, the camp meeting that opened on July 28, 1890 saw over 10,000 attendees at the 'Ten Days Jubilee in the Wilderness.' It featured renowned speakers, Timothy Thomas Fortune and Phebe Ann Hanaford, the most important agenda item being Henry Cabot Lodge's U.S. Senate bill to station overseers at federal elections in the South. The camp assembly voted a resolution of support on July 31 [*Register,* August 1, 1890, p. 3] but, in spite of these efforts, the controversial bill was buried by filibuster and never became law [*Courant*, January 21, 1891, p. 1].

7. The turbulent relationship between the "Upper" and "Lower" portions of what became Orange date back to the founding of the colony when West Haven and North Milford farmers nearly came to blows on several occasions over farmland and borderlines. See Peter J. Malia, *Visible Saints: West Haven, Connecticut, 1648 - 1798* (2009) for more details on West Haven and Orange land disputes.

The Dawn Of A New Century

PART VI.

PUBLIC UTILITIES

TELEPHONE

THE first communication system in the town was a
telegraph line, privately owned and installed between
the homes of Edward L. Clark and his brother, Elias T.
Clark, who lived just over the town line in Woodbridge.
This line was started about 1880, and the Morse system
of dots and dashes was the medium used for their con-
versation.

About 1895 the first telephone system was inaugurated
as a single, private, party line, from the homes of Sylvester
Colburn, Charles S. Clark, and Arthur D. Clark, and
extending to Scobie's store. Later four other circuits were
established in different parts of the town, with a switch-
board in the grocery store.

When the number of subscribers had increased to
forty-eight, this town system was taken over by the
Southern New England Telephone Company on October
13, 1908, and became known as the Orange Telephone
Exchange. The switch-board and central station was
located in the former home of Alpheus N. Merwin.

On January 7, 1938, the Orange Exchange was incorporated with the New Haven Exchange, with 288 telephones at that time. The number of subscribers has stead-
ily increased since that date. At this time the dial system
was inaugurated, doing away with the old custom of
calling the central operator in order to complete a call.
An attractive brick building, which is used as a dial
exchange, was erected on Orange Center Road, opposite
the Center School.

The Orange Water Company

The Orange Water Company was organized as a small, neighborhood system in 1895 by Frank C., Watson S., and Robert J. Woodruff.[1] The source of supply came from a reservoir on Grassy Hill. As the number of subscribers increased, this supply was augmented later by a pipe line from the reservoir of the New Haven Water Company at the Alling's Mills lake. When the Orange Center School was built in 1909, a pipe line was extended to the school as well as to the Green, and fire hydrants were installed in the Center of the Town. A stand pipe and reserve tank were built just north of the Cemetery.

The Orange Water Company was incorporated by a charter obtained from the General Assembly August 29, 1911. The number of users having increased gradually to over seventy-five, the Orange Water Company sold out its interests to the New Haven Water Company in 1938.

The New Haven and Derby Trolley Company

The trolley line connecting New Haven and Derby was started in 1902 and was first opened for service in 1904. The right of way was just south of the Derby Turnpike, running parallel to it for most of the way. This was a double-track system, maintaining half-hourly service. With the increasing use of automobiles, patronage grew less and less. The line was discontinued in 1938, and the tracks and ties were removed. Later this right of way, to a great extent, became the east-bound side of the four-lane highway, over the Derby Turnpike. Bus service, connecting the two towns, succeeded the trolley.

Illumination

The third major change in utilities came in the method of illumination. The means of lighting the homes has gone through a series of evolutionary steps since the early days of the town. First it was the tallow dip, when making the candles was one of the necessary household tasks. Then came kerosene oil, which was a great improve-

116

ment over the flickering candle. It also made possible the use of a lantern, which could be used in the barns. With the advent of the Rochester burner, a much brighter light was obtained.

In 1909 came the third stage of development, when the first lines of the United Illuminating Company were run through the center of the town. Gradually this service was extended to all sections of the town, with street lights installed at strategic corners, as well as a traffic light which is maintained at the busy intersection of Orange Center Road and the Milford Turnpike (or the Boston Post Road, as that part of Route 1 is officially called).

Transportation has changed perceptibly, also. Mention was previously made of the first carriage owned in the town. The first automobile was purchased in 1906 by Frank C. Woodruff, with Ernest Frye acting as his chauffeur.

THE ORANGE FAIR

Following the Grange's successful experiment with agricultural fairs, the Orange Agricultural Society was formed in 1900 to continue the fair in a larger way. Twelve men served as a Board of Directors: Watson S. Woodruff, Walter S. Hine, Arthur D. Clark, Edward L. Clark, Clifford E. Treat, Frank C. Woodruff, Walter H. Beecher, Edward W. Russell, Charles S. Clark, Sylvester G. Colburn, Patrick J. O'Rourke, and Benjamin T. Clark. A few acres of land on the Orange Center Road, just a little south of the Green, were leased from S. D. Woodruff and Sons and the Clark brothers, and a half-mile race track was built with a large grand-stand. A two-story building was erected to hold the vegetable exhibits and the fruit exhibits on the first floor, with the second floor devoted to the women's department. Here were found specimens of fancy work, bed-quilts, and knitted or crocheted articles, besides all kinds of food, canned fruits and vegetables, and many kinds of jellies. Numerous

DIRECTORS OF THE ORANGE FAIR

THE START OF THE BIG PARADE

THE PARADE GETS UNDER WAY

Decorated by Miss Prudence A. Lee

Decorated by Mrs. Watson S. Woodruff

PATRICK J. O'ROURKE AND HIS PRIZE TEAM

ELBERT SCOBIE AT THE WHEEL

121

tents were used in various parts of the grounds to house the exhibits of live stock and poultry, as well as the concessions for food and soft drinks.

A varied program continued throughout the day. In the morning the weight-pulling contest for oxen was a keenly-contested event. The great event of the day was the Grand Parade, starting at 2 p.m. First came the band, then the long strings of live stock, followed by the decorated floats, carriages, or automobiles. There was always much friendly rivalry in arranging the exhibits to appear in the parade. For weeks previous to the opening day, nearly every barn in town held one or more vehicles that were being elaborately decorated with bunting, crepe paper, or other materials, with hundreds of paper flowers.

Following the parade, the great interest of the crowds was centered on the horse racing events. Usually there was a balloon ascension with a parachute drop to give an added thrill. The Fair lasted for three days and was an annual event every September for a number of years. It helped to spread the reputation of the town. The weather was such a deciding factor in the success or failure of the enterprise that all eyes watched the skies as the appointed day drew near.

After 1912 interest in the Fair began to wane, mainly because very inclement weather had interfered with the size of the attending crowd for one or two years, until the Agricultural Society found themselves facing a deficit in the treasury. Finally in 1916, another fair was held, only this time it was held down in the White City section of Savin Rock. This was successful enough to pay all their indebtedness, and after that year the Agricultural Society became only a memory.

LATER CHURCH ACTIVITIES
ORANGE CONGREGATIONAL CHURCH

The young people have always played an important part in the life of the church. Starting about 1880, the group was known as the Hillside Workers, under the leadership of Miss Minnie Clark. They met each Sunday evening at the church for a service, and during the week promoted the social side of the community. After the Christian Endeavor movement gained so much prominence in the country, the Hillside Workers changed their organization into a Christian Endeavor Society in 1887, meeting, as usual, each Sunday night.

The Dorcas Circle of the King's Daughters was organized in January, 1897. Originally it was a little sewing group, formed by Mrs. Clark Stone out of her Sunday School Class.

The Perseverance Circle of the King's Daughters was begun March 19, 1901.

In 1905, when the time arrived to celebrate the one-hundredth anniversary of the founding of the Church, great preparations were made. The building was enlarged by an addition to the north end, approximately 20 by 24 feet, redecorated, and a new carpet procured. The Centennial celebration was a gala occasion lasting three days, from June 30 to July 2, 1905. This was "Old Home Week" for many former residents. Again in 1926 extensive alterations were made. The basement of the church was excavated (a very difficult task), so that rooms were provided to be used as a dining-room as well as a kitchen; also a large addition was added to the west of the building, providing space for Sunday School rooms and a ladies' parlor on the second floor.

January 15, 1940, all of the women's societies connected with the church disbanded, and a new organization was formed, a federation of all the women, young and old, called the Ladies Society of the Orange Congregational Church. It has been so successful that it has clearly demonstrated "in union there is strength."

The Sunday evening service of the present day is conducted by a group of young people, who call their gathering "The Young Peoples Forum." It is open to all boys and girls of high school age. One of the incentives of attending high school when they graduate from the eighth grade is that then they will be eligible to join the Forum. The meetings are opened with a devotional period, followed by a discussion on current topics of the day. The social side is also stressed, as they unite with other groups from neighboring communities.

OTHER CHURCHES

THE CHAPEL OF THE GOOD SHEPHERD

In 1910 Rev. Floyd Kenyon, Rector of Christ Episcopal Church in West Haven, started a little mission in Tyler City. It had a very modest begining, meeting at the home of Mr. and Mrs. Scharff. In 1912 they purchased the old Tyler City schoolhouse, which was no longer in use, and fitted it up as a chapel, which they called The Chapel of The Good Shepherd. Some of the equipment, the altar and the altar rail, came from St. Paul's Episcopal Church in New Haven. The Bishop's chair is one of the oldest in use in this country, as it came from the original Christ Church in West Haven which was built in 1723. Services are held in the Chapel on the first Sunday night of each month, and there are over one hundred members.

Some years later, a parish house was built adjoining the Chapel. This is used for suppers and other social activities.

ST. PAUL'S ROMAN CATHOLIC PARISH

The parish of St. Paul in the Town of Orange was created by Bishop Nilan in 1916. It was to include all that section of the Town of Orange north of the main line of the New York, New Haven and Hartford Railroad.

In 1940 a religious instruction class for Catholic children was conducted at the home of Judge P. B. O'Sullivan. Later that year the children were instructed at the public school. Holding these instruction classes was tried for a time during a recess period, but this system was not too successful.

124

In September, 1944, St. Paul's Parish purchased the former home of Isaac Platt Treat on Orange Center Road, adjacent to the Orange Center School. Since that time, this building has been maintained as a Catholic Community House. At the present time, religious instruction is given to the Catholic children during the noon hour every Tuesday, under the supervision of Rev. John Horgan and some of the Sisters from St. Paul's Convent.

A very active Women's Guild holds frequent meetings here, while a Catholic Men's Club was formed in 1946. Both the Women's Guild and the Men's Club are working to accumulate a fund whereby a Mission Church or a Chapel may be built in the near future, to meet their needs.

In 1902 Mr. and Mrs. Wilson H. Lee came to Orange to live, having bought the farm of Lyman Nettleton, consisting of one hundred acres. Originally they planned to make it their summer home only, but after a few years they liked it so well that they decided to make it their permanent home, which was a very fortunate thing for the town.

Very soon Mr. Lee started the production of high-grade milk with one cow, adding more from time to time until he had a herd of nearly three hundred registered Ayrshire and Jersey cattle. Fairlea Farms milk became known throughout the state as the finest grade of milk. More land was acquired and more crops grown, until the farms comprised eight hundred acres.

Mr. Lee was a very successful printer, a member of the firm of Price, Lee and Adkins Co. of New Haven, which firm eventually became the Wilson H. Lee Company. In 1929 a new building was erected on the Boston Post Road in Orange, near his home, and was equipped with modern machinery for production of high-grade printing. All of the business was then moved to Orange.

In 1912 Prudence A. Lee was married to John R. Demarest, who later became the manager of the printing business. Both Mr. Lee and Mr. Demarest took a very active interest in all town affairs and were a great addition and asset to the town.

Because of the infirmities of advancing years, Mr. Lee was forced to retire from active life. He passed away on May 9, 1948, a few days after celebrating his ninety-fifth birthday. Mr. Lee was a gentleman of the old school, and although not a native, he was as keenly interested in the welfare of the Town as if he had come down from the founding fathers.

LATER MILITARY RECORD

Startling news of war between Germany and France and England dominated the news at this time, but we didn't think it concerned us very much, for Europe seemed so far away. But as events developed, it was found that America was drawn into the conflict.

True to the tradition of the Town, Orange men and women, too, answered the call to the colors.

The names on the Orange Honor Roll, World War I:

Alling, J. Sheldon	Hine, W. Arnold	Patterson, Wm. S.
Bailey, James P.	Jaynes, Harold A.	Peck, Wilbur W.
Barry, Frank E.	Johnson, Wm. S.	Peterson, Levi O.
Bohndorf, Alfred G.	LeBarnes, Ernest L.	Rasmussen, Jacob
Brown, Harold A.	McDermott, George	Rourke, Wm. J.
Buttrick, Nathan LeG.	Selnquist, Albin S.	Scharff, Adrian G.
Buttrick, Phillip L.	Merwin, John J., Jr.	Stevens, Roy R.
Busk, Albert L.	Nelson, Lars C.	Stone, Clifford P.
Crilto, Nicholas	Olson, George R.	Treat, Elbee J.
Clark, Everett B.	Olson, Raymond T.	Treat, Howard B.
Clark, S. Ormund	Otis, Samuel L.	Woodruff, Stiles D.
Czenkus, Tony	Pardee, Wm. D.	Wright, Donald K.
Dahl, Charles H.	Pascucelli, Michael	Wright, Stanley B.
Hayward, Lawrence H.	Pascucelli, Henry	

Charlotte T. Peck—American Red Cross
Catherine H. Woodruff—Y.M.C.A.

MERCHANT MARINE

Andrew, Fields J.	Sperry, Russell F.

When the system of drafting men for the armed services was inaugurated by the Government, Watson S.

126

Woodruff was appointed the Chairman of the Draft Board for Orange.

AMERICAN LEGION

Orange Post, No. 127, American Legion, was officially organized on April 2, 1931, with a membership of twenty-three. The first officers of the Post were:

Commander .... Harry D. Bean
Vice-commander .... Harold A. Brown (D.S.C.)
Adjutant .... George A. Hayes
Finance Officer .... Levi O. Peterson
Historian .... Nelson D. Booth
Judge Advocate .... David N. Torrance
Chaplain .... W. Arnold Hine
Sergeant-at-Arms .... William J. Rourke

The original members appearing on the Charter were:

Patrick B. O'Sullivan	Georgianna Bergen
George Ansel Hayes	Henry Albert Grove
Howard B. Treat	Harold A. Brown
Harry D. Bean	Levi O. Peterson
Clifford P. Stone	Kenyon H. Case
William A. Knight	David N. Torrance
Sandy Kingsbury	Walter R. Scott

W. Arnold Hine

Succeeding Commanders have been:

1932-34 .... Howard B. Treat
1934-36 .... Clark N. Howlett
1936-38 .... Harold B. Forman
1938-40 .... Richard W. Smith
1940-41 ....Joseph G. Lane
1941-42 .... Herbert L. Emanuelson
1942-43 .... William Lake
1943-44 .... Stanley B. Wright
1944-45 .... Joseph Moakley
1945-46 .... George E. Brixner
1946-47 .... Marvin R. Kravet
1947-48 .... Arthur Eberlein
1948-49 .... Chester Hansen

At a competitive drill of the New Haven Grays (Company A, 102nd Infantry), held on May 13, 1931, the Distinguished Service Cross was awarded to two members, one of whom was Harold A. Brown.

The citation reads:

"Harold A. Brown (Army Serial Number 64798), formerly private, first class, Company F, 102nd Infantry, 2*th Division, American Expeditionary Forces. For extraordinary heroism in action in the vicinity of Chavignon, France, on the night of Frebruary 28, 1918. Private Brown was a member of a working party detailed to string barbed wire well out in front of the advance post. His party encountered a violent enemy barrage which protected enemy assault troops. Private Brown helped to fight off the enemy, and with rare coolness and daring continued to pass back and forth through the hostile barrage collecting our men and assisting in the reorganization of the party."

The award was presented by Major James A. Sarratt, U.S.A., D.O.L., representing Major General Fox Connor, Commanding 1st Corps Area.

Captain Howard B. Treat won the Purple Heart for injuries received in action at Rambocourt, France, February 8, 1918.

Private Levi O. Peterson received the Purple Heart with oak-leaf cluster, July 23, 1918, at Chateau Thierry, also on October 27, 1918, in the Argonne, as a member of Company F, 102nd Infantry, Yankee Division.

The present membership of the Orange Post is nearly one hundred. The Post is interested in village improvement and particularly sponsors the work of 4-H boys' clubs and the Boy Scouts. It also takes a very active part in the annual observance of Memorial Day in the Town of Orange.

CONNECTICUT STATE GUARD

Company I, Second Regiment, Connecticut State Guard, was formed in Orange in the Spring of 1917. There were sixty-four members in the Company, with the following officers:

Captain	Robert J. Woodruff
1st Lieutenant	Alexander O. Coburn
2nd Lieutenant	Willis N. Buttrick

Weekly drills were held in the Assembly Hall of the Orange Center School, with a room used as an Armory. Each member of the Company was trained as an expert in military signaling. The Company was fully uniformed and equipped, and took part in many regimental parades. One summer encampment was held at Yale Field. The Company's activities continued until the Winter of 1919.

DIVISION OF THE TOWN

There always seemed to be arguments between the northern and southern parts of the Town. At the special Town Meeting held at William Woodruff's Tavern on May 22, 1848, when they voted to build a town hall on the Milford Turnpike, they also "took into consideration the expediency of dividing said Town of Orange in two towns." This vote was passed unanimously in the affirmative, with the instruction that a petition to this effect be submitted to the next session of the General Assembly. Whether said petition was ever presented to the Legislature is not known, for no further reference is ever made to it in the Town Meeting Journal. On January 21, 1903, there was a special meeting to consider the division of the Town. A committee, composed of Charles F. Smith, John Brown, John F. Barnett, Wellington M. Andrew, and Stiles D. Woodruff, submitted an adverse report. The motion to present a petition to this effect to the General Assembly was lost.

However, a tentative charter, creating the City of Orange, was passed by the General Assembly in 1907. This was a very lengthy document setting forth the duties of every branch of a city's government, but holding the restriction that it would not become effective unless it was accepted by the voters of the Town at a special election, called for that purpose, September 5, 1907. The result of this referendum was that it was defeated in both voting districts.

The same subject came up again in 1910, and a committee of ten was appointed to consider the proposition.

On October 16, 1916, a resolution was passed to establish a commission of twelve to draft a new charter for the

129

Town of Orange. On May 14, 1921, a special meeting was held to consider creating a town out of the Orange Center School District. This plan was opposed by West Haven. However, this was consummated by the special act of the General Assembly of June 24, 1921. Charles R. Treat, who was a State Senator at that session of the Legislature, introduced (and succeeded in having passed) the bill which separated Orange from West Haven. This act provides that the division of the property rights and obligations of the former Town of Orange should be made by the Selectmen of both Orange and West Haven, working together. For this purpose, twenty-two joint sessions were held, and a complete agreement was reached in regard to all matters excepting the location of the boundary lines between the two Towns. The division act provides that the old Town of Orange shall comprise the territory lying west of the Northern and Western School Districts, which is the same as that comprised by the Orange Center School District. Only one boundary stone was found along the entire line, namely, on the south side of the Derby Turnpike. At the annual Town Meeting in 1905, territory was taken from the Northern and Western School Districts and put into the Tyler City District. This line having become fixed and long accepted in the manner above described, the Orange Board believed it had become legally established beyond the power of the two Boards to alter it. The Orange Board believed that the line adopted by the Town Meeting of 1905, until changed by competent authority, is still the true line between the two Towns. The basis of division between the two Towns, as provided by the Division Act, was on the grand list of the year 1920.

The officers elected for the new Town of Orange were:
Selectmen: Charles R. Treat, Edward L. Clark, Clifford E. Treat
Town Clerk: Arthur D. Clark
Treasurer: William T. Andrew
Tax Collector: Irving A. Andrew
Board of School Visitors: Chairman, Frank G. Baldwin

Though Orange is considered a small town, there are thirty-three towns in the State which have less acreage than Orange. Some of these are rated as cities. Of the 169 towns in the State, there are 66 having less population than Orange. There had not been a new town created in the State of Connecticut for almost fifty years, and there has not been any new town in the twenty-five years since Orange and West Haven were made separate Towns. Compared to the rates in other towns in the State, the tax rate of seventeen mills is very low, and the Town has no indebtedness.

Orange was given the merit award by the University of Connecticut, institute of Public Service, for the best annual report for the fiscal year ending August 31, 1945, in the group of towns from 1000 to 2000 population.

Included in the taxable property of the Town of Orange is an island in the Housatonic River. It is called Wooster Island and contains five acres of pasture land located just south of Two-Mile Island.

The latest Grand List of the Town is $8,179,640.00.

Notes

[1] The Orange Water Company was a Woodruff family-owned business. Mary R. Woodruff served as its treasurer as well as a director on the company's board until it was sold to the New Haven Water Company in 1937, not 1938 as Woodruff noted.

Modern Orange

Part VII.

MODERN ORANGE

The Orange Cemetery Association

WHILE the cemetery was first set apart by the Ecclesiastical Society, its maintenance seems to have been assumed, somewhat, by the School Society. Later, the Orange Cemetery Association was formed, and Mr. Isaac Platt Treat was in charge of it for nearly fifty years. Since his death, Albert M. Clark has been the Secretary and Treasurer of the Association. The original size of the cemetery was one-half an acre. This was increased in 1856 by the purchase of an acre, south of the first boundaries. About 1900 it was again enlarged by adding another acre. The members of the Association are to be commended for the excellent way it is maintained, all through the year.

Orange Volunteer Fire Association

After several disastrous fires during the years of 1924 and 1925, it was felt that the old bucket brigade system was inadequate. Accordingly, the Volunteer Fire Association was incorporated on January 9, 1926, with the following fourteen men being the Charter Members:

Terrell, Alton T., Jr.	Knight, William A.	Johnson, George
Hine, George T.	Hine, Frederick J.	Curtis, George M., Jr.
Gardner, John W.	Clark, Benjamin T.	Neal, Chester B.
Harris, Robert	Demarest, John R.	Hall, Clarence L.
Page, Donald	Beebe, James	

At a meeting held in the Orange Town Hall on March 10, 1926, the first officers elected were:

Chief .... William A. Knight
Assistant Chief .... Donald Page
Captain .... Harold Brown
Lieutenants .... William Achtmeyer, Elbert Scobie
Superintendent of Equipment .... James Beebe
Secretary .... George Clark
Treasurer .... John R. Demarest
Executive Committee .... Fred Hine, John Gardner

After a very successful demonstration, a Seagrave pumping engine and a thousand feet of hose were purchased. The abandoned Railroad Station was secured and remodeled to serve as a Fire House. To raise funds, annual carnivals were held. The first carnival, August 25 to 27, netted the Association $2,825. The next year showed a profit of $2,779, and the third carnival, in 1929, made $2,406. Owing to the epidemic of infantile paralysis, no carnival was held in 1931.

Then came the failure of the West Haven Bank & Trust Company, where all the funds were deposited.

In 1935, with the backing of the town, funds were furnished by the Government, the Town, and the Fire Company to purchase land from the Clark brothers on Orange Center Road, and the present Fire House was constructed as a W.P.A. project. In 1936 additional equipment was purchased, which has made an outfit of which the whole Town is proud. In fact, the members of the Orange Department, with their new apparatus, made such a fine showing that they were awarded the trophy for being the best-appearing company in a parade of the State Firemen's Association.

Chief William A. Knight continued to head the association until 1945, when Christian Winkle succeeded him as Chief. The loyalty of the members, and the alacrity with which they respond to the siren's call, are appreciated by every citizen of the Town. They have done much valiant work. There are now 60 active members and 102 associate members. John R. Demarest was Treasurer for several years and was succeeded in 1945 by Frederick Ross.

FIRST FIRE HOUSE AND THE PRESENT FIRE HOUSE

Continuing the Orange School System

After 1860 they discontinued having general school society meetings, each district taking care of its own business as the occasion demanded. Each district had a district chairman and was under the supervision of a board of visitors, who made periodical inspection of the work done and offered suggestions. In 1873 the Tyler City district was created, and a new schoolhouse was built the following year.

About this time, a private kindergarten was conducted by a Mrs. Newcomb in the house now occupied by Benjamin T. Clark. At a Town Meeting held October 5, 1874, it was voted that the school year should consist of thirty-eight weeks, which has always been in force since that time.

On October 7, 1878, they voted that the sum of $1,500 be taken from the Town Treasury and used to erect a building at Orange Center, for a high school and for public purposes. The old Academy was then sold to Leverett B. Treat, who moved it down to a place in back of Mr. Miller's store, where it stood until it was destroyed by fire. The new schoolhouse and town hall was then built on the site of the old Academy.

The five district schools all continued to function along the regular lines, with the stipend for the teachers increasing a little, until in 1900, a teacher was paid ten dollars per week. In 1909 the system of district schools was abolished, and the present school was built. The land on which the school stands was donated to the Town by Frank C. and Watson S. Woodruff.

The Building Committee was composed of the following persons:

Charles R. Treat	Mrs. Benjamin M. Wright
Wilson H. Lee	Wellington M. Andrew
Robert J. Woodruff	Watson S. Woodruff
Bela M. Alling	Arthur D. Clark
Michael E. Tracy	Walter S. Hine

138

ORANGE CENTER SCHOOL

—*Photo by Jonathan Rogers*

This building contains four classrooms, two grades in a room. The children were brought to this central school by four horse-drawn buses, which were put on runners when there was snow. The Town then disposed of the old district schoolhouses. The First District house was sold to Wilson H. Lee, who remodeled it to serve as a dwelling house. It is now occupied by Clark Howlett. The Second District house was sold to Frank C. and Watson S. Woodruff, who moved it a little way north on Ridge Road and raised it up to make a two-story house, which is now occupied by Sumner C. Johnston. The Third District house was bought by Clarence Russell, who made it into a summer home. The Fourth District house was destroyed by fire. Tyler City schoolhouse was purchased by Christ Episcopal Church of West Haven, and is maintained as a chapel.

In 1925 it became necessary to enlarge the building by adding four more rooms, completing the building as it is at the present time. John Hinchliffe was Superintendent of Schools for almost 20 years, and was succeeded in 1945 by Miss Mary Tracy. The control of the school was under a School Committee until 1931, when the Board of Education was created.

The minimum age for entrance to the school was set at six years. However, if a child's birthday falls between September and October 31, he may begin at the opening of school in September.

In 1935 the Harris house, which was adjacent to the school grounds, was purchased by the Town and moved across the street. This land, enlarged by the addition of some property bought from Henry Clark, was turned into an athletic field.

The horse-drawn buses gave way in a few years to motor vehicles. Buses also take the children to the High Schools in New Haven. At the present time, hot cocoa is served during the noon hour to children who stay at the school for lunch. The latest enrollment is about 350 scholars. The teaching staff is composed of the Superintendent, thirteen regular teachers, an art teacher, an instructor in music, and two physical education instructors from Arnold College.

Work is now under way constructing a large addition, which, when completed, will change the appearance of the school completely, and, it is hoped, will provide more adequate accommodations for an up-to-date school with the latest equipment.

The Town Court

The Orange Town Court was established in 1929, with Robert J. Woodruff serving as the first Judge and David N. Torrance acting as Prosecutor. These same officers served until 1937, when Herbert L. Emanuelson became the Judge. He was followed by John B. Grant, who was succeeded by Spencer Hoyt. Mr. Torrance held the office of Prosecutor for twenty years. The present officers are Judge Thomas O'Sullivan, with John McHugh as Prosecutor. Regular sessions of the court, held each week, dispose of much business.

The Orange Police Department

When the Town Court was established, it did away with the old system of Justices of the Peace and fees. According to the Statutes, the First Selectman was considered the Chief of Police, unless he chose to appoint a Constable to serve in that capacity. Therefore, Charles E. Stevens was appointed to that position, and served as Chief of Police until 1935, when he was succeeded by Carl A. Peterson.

By charter from the Assembly, the Orange Police Department was incorporated, and on July 1, 1939, Mr. Peterson officially became Chief of Police, with Joseph Cummings as First Assistant. This Department is under control and jurisdiction of the Board of Selectmen, who appoint all officers. No regular salaried officer on said police force shall have any other gainful occupation. All fees taxed in any court in any criminal proceeding in favor of any police officer except supernumerary officers serving without compensation arising out of the performance of their duties as members of the police depatrment, shall be paid to the Treasurer of the Town. On January 1, 1947, this force was augumented by the appointment of six supernumeraries.

A Police Station is maintained on the Milford Turnpike, or, as it is officially known, the Boston Post Road, U. S. Route No. 1.

ORANGE PUBLIC HEALTH ASSOCIATION

In the early days of the Town, no such thing as a trained nurse was known. If there was serious illness in a family, and the mother needed help, some of her kind neighbors would come in, giving the benefit of their practical experience rather than expert training. In 1925 Willis N. Buttrick was appointed Health Officer, serving both Orange and Milford for a few years. The committee included Mrs. John R. Demarest and Mrs. P. B. O'Sullivan. In 1930 a nurse from the Derby Visiting Nurse Association came to the school once a week. The next year it was voted to have a public health nurse in the school for half-time service every day. Miss Johanna Mueller, R.N., was the first nurse, followed in 1933 by Mrs. Magdalene Fox, R.N.

At a Town Meeting in 1936, they voted to appropriate sufficient funds to employ a full-time health nurse, which position Mrs. Fox has filled since that time.

Each year at the holiday season, the Association assists in selling Christmas seals. Eighty-five per cent of the proceeds is retained for community care, to be used for X-Ray picturse and extra care for anyone afflicted with tuberculosis. Orange is one of a very few towns whose health department is included in the annual town budget; therefore, no extra drive for funds is necessary. On the death of Mr. Buttrick in 1938, Dr. Allan Poole was appointed Health Officer. Each August a pre-school inspection and inoculation is conducted.

The present officers of the Association are: President, Mrs. Harold Wardle; Secretary, Mrs. Floyd Lindley; Treasurer, Mrs. Harry Olsson.

RECREATION

For a small town, Orange is well supplied with golf clubs, as it has three within the limits of the town. Race Brook Country Club, the oldest and largest golf course in the town, was organized in 1912. One hundred and forty-seven acres of land were purchased, and work on the course and the Club House was actively begun. The grand opening was July 4, 1913. The organizing President was Rollin S. Woodruff, who was promptly succeeded by Frank C. Woodruff. The limit of membership was soon reached, causing a badly congested course on general playing days, such as Saturdays, Sundays, and holidays.

In 1923 it was decided to enlarge the course by adding eighteen more holes. One hundred and twenty-eight more acres were bought, and after the full eighteen holes were completed, Race Brook became the only Country Club in New England to offer thirty-six holes to its membership. Robert D. Pryde was the first Professional of the Club in 1912, and served in that capacity for about thirty years.

ORANGE HILLS GOLF CLUB

On the maps of Tyler City (as it was hoped it would become) was a section marked "The Park." This is on a rolling hillside, with a marvelous view, but it remained in its native condition until 1923, when a group of men acquired the property, consisting of eighty-five acres, and laid out a nine-hole golf course on it. This venture did not prove very profitable. As the years passed, these gentlemen lost the property through foreclosure proceedings, and it was acquird by Mr. George H. Woodward,

143

who became sole owner. This course is run on the system of a municipal golf course, without regular membership, but players using it pay daily greens fees, and all guests are welcome.

Due to the very sudden and untimely death of Mr. Woodward, recently, the club is being maintained by his estate, with a manager in charge.

WEPAWAUG GOLF COURSE

This club was started in 1930, and most of its members are residents of Milford. It is known as an eighteen-hole course, although only thirteen holes have really been completed. The land is the property of the Associated Seed Growers and of Walter E. Clark, and is leased to the Club for a very nominal sum on the basis of a long-term lease. There are approximately eighty acres, with a club house on a hillside, commanding a fine view of the surrounding country. The Club has a membership of about one hundred and twenty-five members.

ORANGE ATHLETIC CLUB

Much interest is shown in the Orange Athletic Club by the youth of the town. A baseball team and a football team are maintained, and have many exciting games with rival teams from the nearby towns. Their practice field is the athletic field at the Orange Center School.

CEDAR CREST SUMMER CAMP

The facilities of the Wepawaug River, which used to be used for mills or factories, are now confined, exclusively, to recreation and health-building. A children's camp, owned and operated by the Interservice Clubs Committee of New Haven and supervised by the New Haven Park Commission, occupies thirty-seven acres on both sides of the river. The project was started in 1926, and each year has seen additions of buildings and equipment, until at the present time there are six year-round

144

THE ATHLETIC FIELD

The SWIMMING POOL

145

THE RUSTIC BRIDGE

THE PICNIC TABLE

cabins, each arranged to accommodate eight campers, nine summer cabins, a recreation hall, four eating-shelters, an athletic field, a Camp-director's cabin, eight fireplaces, and a dam which provides an excellent swimming pool. The age for campers is 17 years, but adults are accommodated in week-end groups. The latter provision makes it possible for many girls who work in factories and who live in over-crowded tenements to have at least a few days of fresh air and fun.

There is no charge for camping facilities; all the camper need bring is food, and a stay of two weeks is permitted. Because they took away one of the popular "swimming holes" of the young people of Orange, arrangements have been made whereby the visitors vacate the pool for a couple of hours daily, and then the residents of Orange take over in goodly numbers.

Orange Riding Stables

The horse, which used to be a necessity, has disappeared from our streets, excepting as it is used for recreation. The Orange Riding Stables are maintained on the former Halliwell property to offer this kind of exercise to lovers of this sport.

VARIOUS ORGANIZATIONS

Red Cross

The Orange Branch of the New Haven Chapter of the American Red Cross was started just prior to the first World War, and did much very active work under the leadership of the Chairman, Mrs. Benjamin M. Wright, during the War. After an interim of a few years, the Branch was re-organized in 1937, when Mrs. Allan K. Poole became the Chairman. All through the years of World War II, the Town Hall was taken over for one or two days every week by this very busy group of women, featuring surgical dressings and production work of all kinds.

The Orange Branch had a unique experience during the latter part of 1943, when one of the large industries in New Haven asked the volunteer workers to help them fill a rush order for a secret blackout garment, to be used by fighter pilots. All of the workers, sworn to secrecy, set to work in the Town Hall, and with daily work-sessions, finished their assignment in six working days, which was just one-third of the time set by the factory representative. The blackout suits were assembled at the factory and immediately flown to England, under the personal supervision of said factory representative. The Branch later received a generous check for their efforts, which was sent directly to National Headquarters for use in foreign war relief.

In September, 1945, Mrs. Stanley B. Wright succeeded Mrs. Poole as Chairman.

ORANGE GARDEN CLUB

On March 21, 1930, a few women who were garden lovers met in the home of Mrs. Oliver E. Nelson and formed the Orange Garden Club. The object of the organization is to create interest in gardens in general, and to promote the idea of village improvement and conservation of the beautiful in nature.

SCOUTS

An active troop of Boy Scouts has been maintained for several years, carrying out the principles and program of that most worthy organization. The Cub Scouts take in the younger boys who have not yet reached the age of twelve years but want to get in training for better work when they can be real Scouts. They have had capable leaders who are an inspiration and an incentive for good, serious work.

GIRL SCOUTS

The Orange Troop of Girl Scouts is also doing fine work under the leadership of Mrs. Frederick Lutz, Mrs.

148

George D. Whitney, Mrs. Kenneth Wetherby, and Mrs. William D. Pardee.

BOYS' 4-H CLUB

The Boys' 4-H Club, sponsored by the American Legion, having a membership of twenty-five, is about the largest club of its kind in the State. The age limit of members is from 10 to 20 years. Everett B. Clark is the Senior Supervisor. The scope of their activities is varied, and their interest in various competitions is state-wide. Several of the boys have been awarded the State Prize in the different classes. In 1946 they won permanent possession of the Baldwin Plaque, having won it for three consecutive years. This trophy was given by Arthur L. Baldwin of Milford when he was State Commander of the American Legion. It is awarded, annually, to the best Legion sponsored 4-H Club in the State.

GIRLS' 4-H CLUBS

The Girls' 4-H Clubs are sponsored by the Orange Parent-Teacher Association. The girls are divided into smaller groups, with a teacher for each group. They receive instruction in sewing, cooking, canning, and general home-making efficiency.

Late in August, each year, the boys' and girls' 4-H Clubs hold an exhibition, showing their achievements during the year. These exhibitions cover so many departments that they are almost an agricultural fair.

PARENT-TEACHER ASSOCIATION

The Orange Parent-Teacher Association was established in 1943. It is composed of both fathers and mothers, who are vitally interested in the welfare of the public schools. At each meeting a prize is given to the Grade having the largest number of parents present. Besides sponsoring the 4-H Girls' Clubs, they assist the Public Health Association in serving hot cocoa to the scholars of the Orange Center School at lunch time.

149

THE ORANGE WOMAN'S CLUB

The Orange Woman's Club was formed in 1943 by Mrs. J. Harold Steed, who served as its first President. It is affiliated with the Connecticut State Federation of Women's Clubs; and while it is one of the smallest Clubs in the Federation, it was honored in May, 1947, by being chosen the "Club of the Month" by the General Federation of Women's Clubs, with national headquarters in Washington, D.C., for outstanding interest in foreign relief work.

MILFORD TERCENTENARY

The three-hundredth anniversary of the founding of the Town of Milford was celebrated in an elaborate manner lasting a whole week, August 20 to 26, 1939. Very appropriately, many Orange citizens joined in the festivities.

In the grand parade on August 26, a float was entered in the name of the Town of Orange, and was decorated by Mrs. Walter S. Hine and Mrs. George T. Hine. Said float was awarded the first prize, which was a handsome silver loving cup. This cup is on display in the Orange Fire House.

WILBUR CROSS PARKWAY

Since automobiles have become the principal means of transportation, the demand for better roads was imperative, and each year has seen improvements on the highways. The greatest change came in 1940 to 1941, which culminated in transforming one whole section of the town into a beautiful parkway system, which joins the Merritt Parkway at the Housatonic River.

The Wilbur Cross Parkway stops now at the Derby Turnpike, but it will soon be extended around New Haven and on through the State. Making a four-lane road of the Derby Turnpike has greatly improved that thoroughfare, which connects with the Parkway.

LEWIS BRADLEY HOUSE

(See pages 57 and 101)

After War was declared on December 8, 1941, Orange sprang into action with all the other towns of the State. An airplane spotter tower was erected in Clarence Hall's back-yard and was manned by faithful volunteers, day and night, through all kinds of weather. This service was continued until the Government decided such service was no longer necessary. A report center was maintained in the Town Hall, on a twenty-four hour schedule. The town met every demand that was required, with patriotic fervor.

Orange has come a long way in the last one hundred and twenty-five years. If, as Emerson said, "the use of history is to give value to the present hour and its duty," then this simple word-picture of the past is a challenge and an incentive to the youth of the present to continue to weave the pattern that was so carefully started long ago.

Appendix and Bibliography

APPENDIX AND BIBLIOGRAPHY

Register of the inhabitants of North Milford begun in 1804, when the Society was organized, and continued by Rev. Erastus Scranton:*

Gideon *Alling*, March 16, 1755; Sarah, July 5, 1761; Jared, November 7, 1782; Sally, September 6, 1785; Lyman, January 3, 1788; Eleanor, June 23, 1790; Thomas, M . . . . 8, 1795; Rebecca, May 29, 1797; Julia Smith, July 6, 1799; Eunice, December 13, 1801. (This family moved into the State of New York.)

Elias *Andrew*, died December 22, 1822; Huldah *Rogers*; Elizabeth, died December 9, 1822; Huldah, married to Wm. *Smith*, Jr.; Laura, January 1, 1811, married to Geo. *Umberfield*; Lucy Booth, married to C. Wyllis *Alling*.

Widow Margaret *Andrew*, September 10, 1751; Merwin Andrew, October 3, 1793; Susan Platt, March 17, 1794.

Jonathan *Andrew*.

Barnabas *Andrew*, December 27, 1773, died in New York State; Lydia Sharp, May 30, 1773; Joseph Jonathan, April 20, 1799; Elizabeth, May 9, 1802; Agnes McFee, April 17, 1804; Samuel Beach; Charlotte; John; Samuel; Charlotte, married to David *Isbell*.

Josiah *Boardman*, September 5, 1775; Sarah *Woodruff*, July 5, 1774; Sally, November 19, 1799, died January 28, 1843; Josiah, July 27, 1801; Asa, M . . . . 25, 1803, died October 10, 1805; Harriet, January 2, 1806, died January 9, 1815; Anna Woodruff, September 2, 1808, died May 26, 1809; Asa, M . . . . 15, 1810; Anna Woodruff, July 30, 1812; married to . . . . . *Walker*.

Joseph *Buckingham*, July 12, 1730, died November 23, 1808.

John *Bryan*, February 23, 1754, died December 11, 1840; Mary *Clark*, October, 1754, died March 17, 1815; Elijah; John, June 4, 1781, died April 18, 1824; Mary (Mrs. Joseph *Stone*); Richard; Mira Richardson, married to A. *Kilborn*.

Abijah *Brown*; *Sanford*.

Isaac *Buckingham*; *Belden*; Nancy, married to Wm. *Durand*.

Hervey *Brunson*, February 21, 1774; Fanny, December 27, 1779; Clarissa, August 10, 1799; Miriam, M . . . . 3, 1801; Susan, February 5, 1803; Hervey Denis, February 1, 1805.

Joseph *Buttrick*; Eliza Maryan *Sharp*; Joseph, October 2, 1797; Asa, May 22, 1799; Maryann, May 21, 1803; Jared, April 19, 1805; Enos, J . . . . 5, 1807; Wyllis, February 24, 1809; Maria, April 27, 1811. (This family removed to Massachusetts.)

Harriet *Belden*; Nancy *Belden*.

John *Buttrick*, February 10, 1771; Mary *Stewart*, October 2, 1777;

---

* Subsequent corrections to Scranton's list have been made by Harlan R. Jessup in *Connecticut Ancestry*, February 2007 and May 2007, Vol. 49, Nos. 3 & 4.

Margarette, July 31, 1799; Nathan, October 19, 1801; Clarissa, February 2, 1804; David, May 9, 1806; Esther, July 15, 1808; Mary Naomi, December 6, 1810.

Elias *Clark*, Esq., October 30, 1752; Abigail *Clark*, December 14, 1754; Elias, October 15, 1781; Abigail, April 25, 1785, died September 16, 1824; Sarah, October 9, 1786 (Mrs. Nehemiah Clark); Luke, March 16, 1789; Esther, December 23, 1791; Alpheus, March 17, 1795.

Benjamin *Clark*, January 9, 1738; Sarah *Rogers*, September 20, 1750; Nathan, May 16, 1784.

Benjamin *Clark*, Jr., August 18, 1779; Susanna *Treat*, January 4, 1786; Susan, May 9, 1807, married to Dr. J. M. *Colburn*; Clarissa, married to Treat *Clark*; Benjamin T.; Charlotte; Mary, January 1, 1827.

Isaac *Clark*, August 22, 1757; Susanna *Smith*, December 19, 1767; Polly, September 23, 1784; Isaac, September 26, 1786; Merrit, February 4, 1788; Elon, May 12, 1792; Almon, November 29, 1797; Alvin, December 31, 1800; Keturah *Smith*, August 18, 1789, married to Merrit *Clark*; Susannah *Smith*, January 14, 1792, married to Mr. *Prudden*; Oliver *Smith*, November 4, 1797; Lyman *Smith*, April 28, 1800; Cynthia *Clark*, February 9, 1807; Elizabeth Ann, March 16, 1808, married to Dr. *Allen*; Sarah, married to Albert F. *Miles*.

Nehemiah *Clark*, May 15, 1747, died January 2, 1805; Anna *Platt*, May 8, 1754, died July, 1820; Nehemiah *Clark*, January 13, 1784, died January 11, 1820; (adopted son and her two daughters) Sarah *Camp*, July 25, 1791, married to Abel *Peck*; Sybel *Camp*, May 1, 1795, married to Lemon *Stone*.

Lewis M. *Churchill*, November 18, 1804; killed November 27, 1816.

Enoch *Clark*, December 23, 1747, killed by lightning; Enoch, November 14, 1775; Joseph, June 6, 1782; Richard, October 10, 1789.

Major Samuel *Fenn*, September 27, 1746; Hannah, December 23, 1757; Sally, August 23, 1784, married Enoch *Clark*, Jr.; Lorinda, August 24, 1780, married Nathan *Hall*; Benjamin, March 18, 1778; Cornelia, July 22, 1787.

Samuel *Fenn*, Jr., died at Plymouth, January 14, 1812; *Fowler*; Hart.

Benjamin *Fenn*; Comfort *Fowler*; Benjamin; Fowler; Sarah; Alfred; Nathan, September 24, 1799; Lucinda; Jonathan Fowler; Elmina; Hannah Bryan, May 28, 1808; Clement Comfort; Edward Mills, 1812, died September 11, 1813. (Family moved to Tallmadge, Ohio.)

Peck *Fenn*, February 28, 1768, died at Tallmadge, Ohio, 1824; Urania *Durand*, November 23, 1769; Miranda, November 3, 1794, died March 11, 1796; William Peck, May 1, 1796; Miranda, January 1, 1798; Harvey, December 7, 1799; Joseph, M . . . . 2, 1802; Clarinda,

April 22, 1804; Eliza, April 12, 1806; Sereno, July 8, 1809; Samuel Andrew.

Widow Content *Fowler*, September 12, 1740, died June 19, 1821; Jonathan, August 31, 1771; Hannah, December 28, 1779, married John *Bryan*, Jr.

Josiah *Fowler*, April 21, 1777, died February 17, 1829; Rebecca *Clark*, November 12, 1777; Sally, September 28, 1802, married Asahel *Clark*; Josiah Wales, December 8, 1804; Nathan Clark, March 26, 1807; Emeline Mary, July 5, 1809, married Samuel *Clark*; Jonathan Stiles; Rebecca; Charlotte Clark, married David *Beecher*.

William *Fowler*, July 22, 1732, died February 17, 1809; Eunice *Baldwin*, 1736, died March 16, 1808; Susanah, June 9, 1777, married David *Johnson*; Polly Hotchkiss, February 1, 1780.

Edmund R. *Fowler*, February 25, 1770; Sarah Northrup, February 20, 1779; Albert Miles (adopted son) August 12, 1808; Curtis Summers, July 16, 1793.

Captain John *Gunn*, December 31, 1765, died August 22, 1826; Martha *Treat*, February 7, 1771; Martha Tomlinson, August 3, 1792.

John *Hine*, September 29, 1750; Susannah *Johnson*, July 18, 1762; Urania, November 9, 1786; John, April 18, 1788; Pamela, April 24, 1790, married Mr. *Miller*; Susannah, February 21, 1792, married Shem. *Stebbins*; Esther, M . . . . 1, 1796; Samuel Arnold, April 12, 1798; Widow Sarah *Hine*; Lewis *Churchill*, November 18, 1804.

Joseph *Hine*, September 12, 1752, died August 3, 1822; Sarah *Baldwin*, August 4, 1763, died May 27, 1823; Mary, July 13, 1784, married Philo *Baldwin*; Andrew Parson, May 21, 1786; Eunice, April 2, 1788; Lois, December 8, 1790, married Captain *Potter*; Anna, December 11, 1792; Sarah, January 17, 1795, married Johnson *Camp*; Martha, January 2, 1798; Assenah, December 21, 1800; Hervey Moses, May 17, 1803; Clarissa, M . . . . 30, 1805.

Aaron *Hine*, M . . . . 14, 1732, died October 7, 1813; Aaron *Hine*, Jr., M . . . . 25, 1777; Bithia *Hitchcock*, June 19, 1784; Harriet, July 2, 1805; Julia, December 11, 1809. (This family moved to Ohio.)

Abraham *Hine*, November 16, 1775; Abigail *Elton*, November 16, 1775; Alvin, July 16, 1797; William, July 23, 1801; Margarette, November 12, 1803; Dan, May 22, 1806; Denis, April 11, 1808. (This family moved to Ohio.)

Nathan *Hall*, November 4, 1781; Elvira, August 4, 1806; Nathan Fenn, January 2, 1809.

Belden *Hodge*.

Jesse *Hodge*, April 29, 1780; Nancy *Hooker*, 1784; Nancy Selina, April 10, 1806; Widow Sarah *Hodge*, February 28, 1742; Martha *Hodge*, October 19, 1771.

David *Johnson*, June 21, 1771; Susannah *Fowler*, June 9, 1777; Widow Susannah J., December 10, 1730; Lucy.

William *Johnson*, April, 1790; Chloe *Johnson*, August 27, 1792; Martin Ford, Abigail Law.

David *Lambert*, December 13, 1731, died November 8, 1815; Martha *Northrup*, July 21, 1737; Ephraim Northrup, January 3, 1760; Sarah, October 28, 1763; Mabel, June 17, 1774; Edward Allen, August 3, 1780; Benjamin Lot, September 29, 1782.

John *Lambert*, November 20, 1770; Esther *Woodruff*, December 22, 1779; John Lot, March 10, 1801; Esther Maria, November 23, 1802, died January 11, 1811; Betsey Maretta, September 12, 1804, died February 28, 1817; Mary Emeline, November 30, 1806; Hetta Matilda, May 1, 1809; Esther Maria, January 20, 1811, married Calvin A. *Treat*; Mabel L., June 25, 1814; Betsey Maria, June 30, 1816.

Benedict Arnold *Law*, December 31, 1740, died November 19, 1819; Henrietta *Gibbs* (2nd wife) 1767; Richard Bryan, July 12, 1780; Andrew, September 10, 1782; Sarah Bryan, October 9, 1785, married Eben. *Johnson*; Lyman, October 9, 1788; John Gibbs, July 12, 1791, died September 29, 1816; Hervey, July 22, 1794; Esther, January 15, 1797, married to Fowler *Fenn*; Wyllis, April 8, 1800, died August 19, 1819; Henrietta, August 19, 1804; Abigail Andrew, May 29, 1807.

Amos *Mallory*, August 15, 1770; Sarah *Hodge*, January 8, 1765; Lyman, October 24, 1794; Patty Maria, June 19, 1798; Cornelius, November 24, 1799, died November 16, 1805; Minerva, January 23, 1806; Patty Maria, July 23, 1803.

Amos *Nettleton*, November 1, 1771; Comfort *Nettleton*, October 28, 1783 (his sister).

David *Nettleton*, November 21, 1778; Mehitable *Sanford*, June 11, 1781; Patty Maria, June 3, 1802; Sally Smith, November 1, 1803, married David *Mallory*; Hannah Treat, October 20, 1805; David, January 30, 1808; Charlotte, December 6, 1809, married Jeremiah *Woodruff*; William Hervey, September 7, 1811; Marilla, October 11, 1813, married David *Lillingston*; Nancy Eliza, June 22, 1816, married Henry *Cornwall*; Emily, married Henry *Baldwin*.

Isaac *Nettleton*; Elizabeth *Burwell*; Isaac; Susannah.

Oliver *Nettleton*, adopted son of Joseph *Buckingham*.

Samuel *Prudden*, January 16, 1743, died July 12, 1819; Samuel, November 25, 1785; Joseph, August 5, 1787; Peter, March 12, 1790; Sally, January 4, 1792, married Anson *Davis*.

Jonathan *Prudden*, died January 10, 1806; Sarah *Clark*, February 10, 1743; Cata *Downs* (adopted child).

Jeremiah *Parker*, January 8, 1758; Sarah *Treat*, December 10, 1751; Andrew, January 4, 1784; Charity, August 11, 1786; Sarah.

March 30, 1789; Jeremiah, June 9, 1791, died July 12, 1812; Nancy, January 19, 1794; Ira, September 19, 1795; Mary Ann, July 4, 1798; Treat, December 25, 1800; Horace, March 27, 1804.

Widow Rebecca *Pardee*, January 2, 1746; (her mother, Mary *Beecher*, died May 21, 1717); Rebecca, April 9, 1768; married Jonah *Dickerman*; Content, November 22, 1769; married Sam. B. *Smith*; Mahitable, November 24, 1777; married Eli *Hull*.

Joseph *Pardee*, 1748; died March 16, 1824; Abigail *Bryan*, 1742, died January 25, 1833.

Joseph *Pardee*, Jr., September 20, 1780, died November 1, 1863; Sarah *Hine*, October 31, 1780, died December 28, 1863; Edwin, October 6, 1805, married Caroline *Prince*, died November 5, 1887; Sidney, May 27, 1810, died November 18, 1891; Merrit, November 29, 1815, died March 28, 1874; Joseph Harvey, October 2, 1818, died April 18, 1868; Sarah Abigail, May 16, 1823, died January 10, 1901.

Richard *Platt*; Margaret *Fowler*.

Asa *Platt*, March 19, 1769; Martha *Woodruff*, February 3, 1770; Mary Ann, December 6, 1791; Enoch Woodruff, November 4, 1793; Martha, May 23, 1796, married Raymond *Baldwin*; Hetty, November 9, 1798; Asa Gideon, June 23, 1801, died May 12, 1832; Esther Maria, January 1, 1804; Marcus, June, 1807, died October 7, 1808; Laura; Lucretia Newhall.

Samuel *Parsons*; Charlotte *Clark*; Jerusha; Aaron Clark; Samuel.

Jireh *Platt*, January 15, 1768; Keturah *Smith*, September 24, 1772; Hannah Smith, September 4, 1792, married J. *Stevens*; Clarissa, July 26, 1794; Keturah, October 16, 1796; Jireh, March 23, 1798; William, June 27, 1799; Hervey, October 18, 1801; Polly Esther, October 31, 1804; Minerva, November 4, 1806.

Jonathan *Rogers*, died March 20, 1821; Elizabeth *Camp*, November 30, 1748.

Jonathan *Rogers*, Jr.; Polly *Treat*, 1785, died January 5, 1867; Julia, September, 1804, married Bela *Alling*; Jonathan Treat, September 2, 1806, married Eliza *Clark*; Jonah, December 21, 1808, married Sarah *Clark* (sister of Eliza); Mary, November 19, 1809, married Fowler *Fenn*.

Joseph *Stone*, January 30, 1756, died December 14, 1811; Sarah *Beech*, November 19, 1766; Joseph, July 16, 1787; Mary, June 21, 1789, married Jeremiah *Rice*; Sarah, M . . . . 25, 1791, married *Tomlinson*; Philemon, January 26, 1794, married Sybel *Camp*; Lanson, April 2, 1798; Dennis Beech, October 6, 1805, married Sarah *Shelton*.

Samuel *Stone*, December 31, 1756; Naomi *Nettleton*; September 26, 1760; William, May 19, 1785; Naomi, March 31, 1792, married Joseph *Prudden*.

Samuel *Stone*, Jr., October 19, 1779; Mary *Woodruff*, May 8, 1782; Sidney Mason, August 8, 1803; Benjamin Woodruff, April 14, 1808.

Richard *Stone*, October 6, 1785; Mahitable *Treat*, November 11, 1786.

William *Smith*, August 24, 1771; Anna *Pardee*, M . . . . 16, 1771; William, September 16, 1801; Salina, May 25, 1804; Josiah Pardee, July 10, 1806; Sidney, December 14, 1808.

Amos *Smith*, July 5, 1781; Phebe *Platt*, February 12, 1786; Merrit Platt, January 6, 1804; Phebe Minerva, November 1, 1806; Sidney, December 6, 1809. (This family moved to Ohio.)

Polly *Stephens*, April 1, 1792; Lena Sanford, married Allen *Umberville*; Hannah Sharp, July 17, 1739.

Asa *Sperry*, February 22, 1769; Eunice *Johnson*, May 9, 1772; Kneeland T., August 7, 1790; Amanda, M . . . . 14, 1794, married E. *Griffen*; Atlanta, July 8, 1795, married E. *Sperry*; Erastus, April 21, 1797; Ransom, May 24, 1799; Isau, December 12, 1801; Asa Ellsworth, April 2, 1804; Eunice, June 25, 1807, married O. *Bradley*; Bennett Wells, October 28, 1809; Adoline, August 28, 1812, married S. Y. *Beach*; Emeline, August 28, 1812. (Adoline and Emeline were twins.)

Joseph *Treat*, January 1, 1738; Rebecca *Downs*, December, 1739.

Joseph *Treat*, Jr., December 21, 1777; Eunice *Newton*, October 1, 1782; Julia Eunice, November 18, 1801, married Elias *Myrrich*; Marietta Newton, July 21, 1803, married Andrew *Treat*; Joseph, January 29, 1805, died November 3, 1805; Joseph Tullar, April 9, 1807; Calvin Austin, November 27, 1809.

Robert *Treat*, Jr., May 25, 1758; Content *Bryan*, May 8, 1760; Robert, January 31, 1785; Charlotte, October 16, 1788; Content, November 16, 1795, married Leverett *Treat*.

Robert *Treat*, Sr., October, 1730, married Mary *Clark*, died August 10, 1807.

Jonathan *Treat*, August 12, 1763; Susannah *Gunn*, July 29, 1764; Susan, January 4, 1785; Jireh, June 23, 1794, married to Sally *Platt*; Jonathan, July 9, 1800, married to Mary *Baldwin*.

David *Treat*, 2d, July 22, 1776; Lidia *Pardee*, January 1, 1788; Samuel Wyllis, October 6, 1801; Mary, November 3, 1803; Isaac Pardee.

Isaac *Treat*, April 7, 1756; Mahitable *Platt*, March 5, 1762; Esther, September 26, 1789, married A. *Clark*; Isaac, April 18, 1795; Nathan, December 29, 1799.

David *Treat*, December 10, 1765; Mahitable *Platt*, April 4, 1771; Leverett, July 3, 1793; David, March 21, 1797; Hetta, March 25, 1799, married to Jonah *Treat*, Jr.; William, May 11, 1802; Mary Merwin,

June 7, 1805, married to Albert *Alling*; Susan, January 10, 1809, married to David *Beecher*.

Widow Anna *Treat*, February 23, ——.

Richard *Treat*, June 20, 1760; Sarah *Smith*, December 3, 1765; Sybel (idiot), November 24, 1787; Selah, June 29, 1793.

John *Treat*, November 7, 1755; Esther *Clark*, August 23, 1771; Eunice, March 20, 1790; John, February 14, 1795; Elizabeth Ann, September 5, 1797, married Alpheus *Clark*; Gerry, January 19, 1799; Andrew, December 22, 1801; Richard Bryan, May 1, 1803; Esther, October 22, 1805; Sidney Clark, December 5, 1806.

Widow Frances *Treat*, Esq., August 16, 1726.

Captain Jonah *Treat*, November 27, 1767; Rebecca *Treat*, May 15, 1770; Frances, February 24, 1792, married Luke *Clark*; Jonah, September 17, 1794, married Hetty *Treat*; Julia Bryan, January 26, 1802; Hervey Hubbard, February 2, 1807; Alfred, March 25, 1809, married Catherine *Clark*; Rebecca Maria, March 7, 1814, married Bryan *Clark*.

Isaac *Treat* (lived there), February 22, 1788.

Samuel *Treat*, August 16, 1760; Sarah *Nettleton* (1st wife), died June 28, 1793; Clarissa *Whitman* (2nd wife), May 30, 1768; Sarah, April 28, 1788, married O. *Nettleton*; Mary, June 5, 1790, married R. *Bryan*; Samuel, March 22, 1795; Oren, Orel (twins), April 21, 1797; Clarissa, October 10, 1800, married to Samuel *Comes*; Calvin, March 13, 1803; Erastus Scranton, April 20, 1805; Almira, October 4, 1807; Esther, married William *Grant*.

Joseph *Umberville*, Novmeber 27, 1759; Bathsheba, April 11, 1766; Allen, March 11, 1788; Belizar Wyllis, September 18, 1795.

Widow Mary *Woodruff*, June 11, 1745; Anna, May 17, 1785, married R. B. *Law*; Anna *Thomas* (who lives in the family); also John *Pardee*, 1760.

Ichabod A. *Woodruff*, January 18, 1777; Sarah *Belden*, October 11, 1778; Enoch, July 24, 1800; William, January 27, 1802; Harriet Belden, June 7, 1804, married Bela *Isbel*; Mary Treat, May 16, 1806, married Andrew *Treat*; Edwin, March 1, 1813; Sarah, April 23, 1815.

Matthew *Woodruff*, December 18, 1743; Esther *Bull*, March 11, 1750; John *Woodruff*, August, 1797; William *Beecher* (a domestic).

Joel *Woodruff*, March 5, 1778; Hannah *Clark*, February 1, 1781; Merit, August 18, 1802; Julia, November 14, 1806, married John *Hawley*.

Nehemiah *Woodruff*, May 24, 1774; Hannah *Jones*, August 6, 1777; Caroline, April 14, 1798; Hannah, February 8, 1800, married David *Treat*, 3rd; Mary Pond, November 14, 1802, married Samuel *Hine*; John, October 6, 1804; Samuel Jones, July 1, 1806; Jeremiah, June 27, 1811.

Families omitted:

Amos *Clark*; Eunice *Clark*; Amos; Selah; Ira; Lanson; Polly *Camp* (assistant), married George *Baldwin*.

Families of Africans and Descendants of the native Indians:

Titus *Ward*; Roswell *Homer*.

Benjamin *Roberts*; Patty *Sharp*; Benjamin; Samuel; Levi; Elijah; Hannah, married J. *Bagden*; Sylvester.

Peter *Myrrich,* 1753; Susannah, August 10, 1763; Sally, May 1, 1794, married Charles *Treadwell*; Molly, September 12, 1796; Peter, October, 1799; Sukey Jane, September 29, 1810; Lois, 1788; Benjamin, 1803.

Molly *Hatchet*, July, 1738; Joseph *Richardson*, October, 1786; Cata, April 9, 1787; Betsey, May 11, 1805, married Francis *Andrus*; Jacob, January 20, 1808; Nancy, January 4, 1810; David, March 5, 1812.

Iamon *Clark*, July, 1794; Charlotte *Clark*, 1804.

SELECTMEN FOR THE TOWN OF ORANGE

1822 John Bryan, Jr., Thomas Painter, Ichabod A. Woodruff, Aaron Thomas, Jr., Lyman Law
1823 Ichabod A. Woodruff, Benjamin Clark, Nehemiah Kimberly
1824 Nehemiah Kimberly, Jesse Alling, Luke Clark
1825 Nehemiah Kimberly, Richard Platt, David Johnson
1826 Alpheus Clark, David Johnson, Eliakim Kimberly
1827 Eliakim Kimberly, Benjamin Clark, Isaac Treat
1828 Eliakim Kimberly, Lyman Law, Lyman Prindle
1829 Josiah M. Colburn, Lyman Law, Lyman Prindle
1830 Lyman Law, Lyman Prindle
1831 Eliakim Kimberly, Josiah M. Colburn
1832 Eliakim Kimberly, David Johnson
1833 Eliakim Kimberly, David Johnson
1834 Eliakim Kimberly, Jesse G. Smith
1835 Eliakim Kimberly, Nathan Merwin, Jesse G. Smith, Solomon Johnson, Nehemiah Kimberley, Lyman Law, Aaron Clark, Jr.
1836 Nathan Merwin, Eliakim Kimberly, Jesse G. Smith, Nehemiah Kimberly, Solomon Johnson, Lyman Law, Aaron Clark, Jr.

1837 Nathan Merwin, Jesse G. Smith, Nehemiah Kimberley

1838 Nathan Merwin, James Reynolds, Jesse G. Smith

1839-40 Nathan Merwin, James Reynolds, Leverett B. Treat

1841-42 Aaron Clark, Jr., Nathan Merwin, James Reynolds

1843 Nathan Merwin, James Reynolds, Albert F. Miles

1844 James Fitts, Nehemiah Kimberley, Albert F. Miles, Aaron Clark, Jr., Silas Thompson

1845 James Fitts, Albert F. Miles, Albert Candee, Benjamin T. Clark, Lucius Stevens

1846 James Reynolds, James Fitts, Albert F. Miles

1847 James Fitts, Albert F. Miles, Enoch Somers

1848 James Fitts, Enoch Somers, Bryan Clark

1849 Albert F. Miles, Bryan Clark, Enoch Somers

1850 Albert F. Miles, Enoch Somers, Bryan Clark

1851 Albert F. Miles, Bryan Clark, William N. Barnett

1852 Albert F. Miles, Edgar Smith, William A. Bronson

1853 William A. Bronson, Edgar M. Smith, Benjamin T. Clark

1854 Edgar M. Smith, Benjamin T. Clark, Dennis B. Stone

1855-56 Benjamin T. Clark, Albert Candee, Dennis B. Stone

1857 Benjamin T. Clark, Hervey W. Painter, Dennis B. Stone

1858 Benjamin T. Clark, Dennis B. Stone, Josiah Culver, Bryan Clark, Silas Pardee

1859 Benjamin T. Clark, Dennis B. Stone, Bryan Clark

1860 Benjamin T. Clark, Isaac Hine, George H. Alling

1861-62 Benjamin T. Clark, Isaac Hine, George H. Alling

1863-66 Benjamin T. Clark, Isaac Hine, Enoch Clark

1867 Benjamin T. Clark, Isaac Hine, George W. Tuttle

1868-69 Benjamin T. Clark, Isaac Hine, Enoch Clark

1870-71 Benjamin T. Clark, Samuel Smith, 2nd, George H. Alling

1872-73 Benjamin T. Clark, Samuel L. Smith, James Graham

1874-75 Benjamin T. Clark, Samuel L. Smith, Elijah E. Benham

1876 Benjamin T. Clark, Samuel L. Smith, Luther Fowler

1877 Benjamin T. Clark, Samuel L. Smith, James Graham

1878-79 Benjamin T. Clark, Samuel L. Smith, David Platt

1880 Samuel L. Smith, Charles F. Smith, Hiram H. Smith

1881-82 George R. Kelsey, Charles F. Smith, David Platt

1883 George R. Kelsey, Isaac P. Treat, David Platt

1884 Edward W. Wilmot, Isaac P. Treat, David Platt

1885 Samuel L. Smith, Isaac P. Treat, David Platt

1886 Samuel L. Smith, Isaac P. Treat, Charles T. Sherman

1887 Charles T. Sherman, Charles F. Smith, Elbee J. Treat

1888 Walter A. Main, Elbee J. Treat, Charles F. Smith

1889 Joseph Andrews, Elbee J. Treat, Andrew D. Thomas

1890 David Platt, Elbee J. Treat, Joseph Andrews

1891-92 Joseph Andrews, William C. Russell, Charles F. Smith

1893 Joseph Andrews, Victor A. King, Charles F. Smith

1894 Joseph Andrews, William C. Russell, Charles F. Smith

1895-96 Walter A. Main, William C. Russell, Charles F. Smith

1897 Walter A. Main, Howard P. Treat, David Platt

1898-99 Walter A. Main, Howard P. Treat, William A. Russell

1900 Walter A. Main, Elford C. Russell, William A. Russell

1901 Walter A. Main, Elford C. Russell, Dennis A. Kimberley

1902-06 Walter A. Main, Elford C. Russell, William A. Russell

1907 Walter A. Main, Elford C. Russell, Joseph Grannis

1908-11 Walter A. Main, Elford C. Russell, Greene Kendrick

164

1912-13 Walter A. Main, Elford C. Russell, Joseph Grannis
1914-17 John Wilkinson, Elford C. Russell, Ray T. Humphrey
1918-19 John L. Sherman, Clifford E. Treat, Joseph W. Grannis
1920 John L. Sherman, Clifford E. Treat, James Hughson
1921-23 Charles R. Treat, Edward L. Clark, Clifford E. Treat
1924 Charles R. Treat, Edward L. Clark, James J. McDermott
1925 Charles R. Treat, William T. Andrew, James J. McDermott
1926-28 Walter S. Hine, William A. Knight, James J. McDermott
1929 Walter S. Hine, William A. Knight, Patrick B. O'Sullivan
1930-35 Walter S. Hine, William A. Knight, Charles F. Treat
1936-41 Walter S. Hine, William A. Knight, Minott A. Smith
1942-45 Walter S. Hine, William A. Knight, Elmer L. Manley
1946 William A. Knight, Charles F. Treat, Elmer L. Manley
1947-49 W. Arnold Hine, Willis Wilkinson, Elmer L. Manley

Special mention should be made here of the long and efficient term as First Selectman which was achieved by Walter S. Hine, who served in that capacity for twenty years, consecutively, with much credit to himself as well as to the Town.

Town Clerks

1822-26 Benjamin L. Lambert
1826-31 Solomon Johnson
1831-34 Lyman Prindle
1834-49 William Woodruff
1849-54 Sydney Pardee
1855-57 J. Seymour Pardee

1858-87   Elias T. Main
1888-92   Walter A. Main
1892-1920 George H. Thomas
1921-1947 Arthur D. Clark
1948-   Howard B. Treat

Of this list, two men have made enviable records as careful and efficient servants of the Town. Elias T. Main served for almost thirty years, and Arthur D. Clark served for twenty-six years.

The list of Orange men in World War II is long and imposing. Some of them volunteered, while others answered the call of their Draft Board. Robert J. Woodruff represented the Town on the Draft Board, and Dr. Allan K. Poole was the Medical Examiner.

The Orange Service Committee, with Mrs. P. B. O'Sullivan as secretary, compiled the following roster:

Frederick H. P. Alford
Donald C. Alford, Jr.
Frederick E. Almquist
Wasil Alshuk
Arthur F. Anderson, Jr.
George A. Archer
Gordon K. Atwood
Herbert S. Barnes
Robert E. Barton
William C. Bergen
Raymond J. Bergman
Wallace Bilinski
John Blanchard
James Blennerhassett
J. David Blennerhassett
Paul Blennerhassett
William L. Blennerhassett
John L. Booth
Arthur Boppert
Walter Boppert
George C. Brixner
Charles W. Brownell
Donald F. Buckholz
Ernest A. Buckholz

Howard W. Buckholz
Joseph J. Buckholz, Jr.
Julius H. Buckholz
John L. Buttolph, Jr.
Kenneth Buttry
Ralph E. Capecelatro
Emerson Carter
Richard L. Chatfield
Constantine Ciola
Edward Ciola
Paul Ciola
Erlon H. Clement
Clayton S. Cole
Charles D. Collins
John J. Collins
Thomas F. Collins
George A. Cook
William R. Couglin
John D. Crowley
Seward R. Crozier
John R. Cuzzocreo
Raymond Cuzzocreo
Frank Czenkus
Joseph F. Cummings

166

Louis F. Diehl
John V. Donchenko
Harold E. Drew, Jr.
Robert S. Drew
Virginia Drew
Fred R. Driscoll
H. Lincoln Dunn, Jr.
Ellsworth A. East
Fred A. East
Arthur G. Eberlein
John W. Fanning
Anthony Farina
Jack A. Farino
Joseph F. Farrell
William Fox
Bernard J. Foyer, Jr.
Grace R. Freeman
Milton E. Freeman
John Aaron Frey
Dwight C. Gager
Richard E. Gager
John W. Gamsby
Carl J. Garborcauskos
James P. Garborcauskos
Walter J. T. Garceau
Colin R. Gemmell
Donald Gemmell
Ian L. Gemmell
William H. Gordon
Fred D. Graham
Anthony Greco
Joseph A. Green, Jr.
Robert T. Grippen
Wilbur B. Grippen, Jr.
Charles F. Hackett
Elmer R. Hackett
Edwin A. Hafner
Harold R. Hafner
Art R. Hamilton
William G. Hankey
Harold B. Hanlon
Paul A. Hanlon
Edward J. Hannon
John C. Healey
William F. Healey, Jr.
James H. Heinz

Paul Hencharyk
Richard Hencharyk
John Hill
Stephen Hill
Thomas C. Hill
William F. Hill
George T. Hine, Jr.
Herbert S. Holland, Jr.
Clark N. Howlett
Joseph L. Hujber
Joseph B. Jankowski
Michael J. Jelasko
Donald Jewell
Frederick L. Johnson
Allan C. Jones
Henry I. Karney
Watson Karney
Francis H. Keefe
James F. Keesler
Charles P. Khoury
John Kiawenis
Ernest C. Kirchberg
Louis J. Kishel
Phillip P. Kishel
Robert A. Knight
Walter Knox, Jr.
Joseph Lanfranco
Phillip Lange
Clayton Leaver
Franklin B. Lewis
Charles S. Lindley
Frederick Loman
Nicholas Loman
Frank Lombardi
Louis Lord
Charles Luce
Bernard Luttenberger
George P. Lyder
Euerle L. Macdonald
John S. Mallory
Alfred W. Marsch
Earl J. Massoth
Joseph Mattei
Arthur E. Mattell
Sinclair B. McClelland
George B. McNamara

167

Wilbur R. Meunier
William F. Mitchell
Walter E. Monck
Robert W. Moran
Alfred Nedovich
Allen W. Neff
Frank A. Nelson
Grant E. Nelson
Lawrence E. Nelson
Alfred C. Neves
Frank Nicoletti
John S. Noble
Wilson P. Noble
Daniel Noon
Rita R. Noon
James Norback
Richard L. Norris
Robert L. North
David Novenstein
William F. Orrell, Jr.
Robert B. O'Sullivan
Angelo Passariello
Louis Passariello
Robert B. Pastorius
Andrew Patterson
Arthur W. Peberdy
Wilfred H. Peberdy
Bennett C. Peckingham
James A. Peckingham
Edward J. Pender
Cyril S. W. Perry
Clifford E. Petersen
Ida M. Peterson
Ruth E. Peterson
Calvin T. Pierson, Jr.
William F. Pilling
Verna Pitts Browne
Waldo W. Plaisted
Allan K. Poole, Jr.
Charles N. Prouty, III
John E. Puska
Victor L. Quentin
Edward Regula
Joseph Regula
Pasquale J. Richitelli
Adam W. Riskiewicz

Maurice Rogers, Jr.
Everett Russell
Frederick H. Russell
Wesley E. Russell
Dominic Salemme
Frank Salemme
Sylvester E. Salemme
Pasquale Savarese
Camille J. Schebell
Harold J. Sclmele
John Y. Short
Raymond A. Silvernale
Charles S. Sims
Earnest Skalsky
Stanley Skalsky
Nicholas Skiba
Charles Smith
David Dean Smith, Jr.
Donald H. Smith
Reginald A. E. Smith
Richard T. Smith
Robert H. Smith
Winthrop F. Smith
Frederick C. Sperry
Leroy R. Sperry
Russell E. Sperry
James E. Steele
Estelle A. Stillman
Kenneth H. Stillman
Malcolm Stillman
Frederick C. Stone
Jerry J. Suller
Thomas W. Tanner
Joseph W. Taraskevich
Peter H. Taraskevich
Harry Taurick
Samuel Taurick, Jr.
Russell E. Thomas
Arthur G. F. Tirrell
Robert Tirrell
William M. Tompkins
Edward S. Tower
Bronislaus Tracz
John C. Tracz
Peter C. Tracz
Joseph I. Tupko

Peter Tupko
Salvatore C. Vespoli
Ervin D. Wachtel
Arthur Wahnquist
Charles C. Wales
Lorin H. Weed, Jr.
Carl H. Weis
Frederick A. Weis
John S. Wheeler, Jr.
George Whitaker
George D. Whitney
Richard D. Williams

George E. Woodruff
Robert J. Woodruff, Jr.
Stiles D. Woodruff, III
Thomas M. Wright
Joseph Yarosh
Merwin Yarosh
Philip Yarosh, Jr.
Walter Yarosh
Homer A. Yates, Jr.
William P. Yates
Anthony Zelinsky
Harry Zuraw

Killed or missing in action:

Lieutenant Frederick E. Almquist
Private First-class Wasil Alshuk
Donald Gemmell, Chief Machinist's Mate, U.S.N.
Wilson P. Noble, U.S.N.
Dominic Salemme

Purple Heart winners:

William Coughlin
Sergeant Ervin D. Wachtel
Sergeant Stiles D. Woodruff, III

BIBLIOGRAPHY

Church Records, 1804-1946, Orange Congregational Church

Orange Ecclesiastical Society, 1804-1929, Minutes of Meetings

Orange School Society Records, 1806-1908

Statistical History of Milford, Erastus Scranton, 1835, Town Clerk's Vault, Milford

Town Meeting Journal, Orange, 1822-1920, Town Clerk's Office, West Haven

Historical Recollections, MSS., Edward L. Clark, Orange

History of the Old Red House, MSS., Henry L. Woodruff, Orange, 1884

Derby Turnpike Journal, 1798-1897

BOOKS

Barber, John W., *Connecticut Historical Collections*, New Haven, 1856

Beers, Frederick W., *Atlas of New Haven County*, New York, 1868

Clark, George T., *History of New Haven County*

DeForest, John W., *History of the Indians of Connecticut*, Hartford, 1853

Dwight, Timothy, *Travels in New England and New York*

Hill, Edwin, *History of New Haven County*

History of Milford, *Tercentenary Edition*, 1939

History of West Haven, 1940

Lambert, Edward R., *History of the Colony of New Haven*, New Haven, 1838

Mitchell, Mary H., *New Haven County, Connecticut*, 3 volumes

Orcutt, *History of Derby*

Osborn, Norris, *History of New Haven County*

Prudden, Lillian E., *Peter Prudden, a Story of his Life*, 1901

Rockey, J. S., *History of New Haven County*, 2 volumes

Treat John H., *The Treat Family Genealogy*, Salem, 1893
Trumbull, Benjamin, *Complete History of Connecticut*, 2 volumes, 1818
Wood, F. J., *The Turnpikes of New England*

NEWSPAPERS

The New Haven Journal-Courier, various dates
The New Haven Palladium, various dates
The New Haven Register, various dates

Index

(This index does not include names in the Appendix).

173

INDEX

175

www.ingramcontent.com/pod-product-compliance
Lightning Source LLC
Chambersburg PA
CBHW032059080426
42733CB00006B/339